1909 Investment Digest
and
1929 Annual Stock Forecast

W. D. Gann

Contents for December, 1909

THE TICKER PUBLISHING COMPANY

2 RECTOR STREET   NEW YORK

WILLIAM D. GANN

THE
TICKER
INVESTMENT AND DIGEST

Investment: The placing of capital in a more or less permanent way, maimly for the income to be derived therefrom.

Speculation: Operations wherein intelligent foresight is employed for the purpose of deriving a profit from price changes.

| Vol. 5 | DECEMBER, 1909 | No. 2 |

William D. Gann

An Operator Whose Science and Ability Place Him in the Front Rank— His Remarkable Predictions and Trading Record.

SOMETIME ago the attention of this magazine was attracted by certain long pull stock market predictions which were being made by William D. Gann. In a large number of cases Mr. Gann gave us in advance the exact points at which certain stocks and commodities would sell, together with prices close to the then prevailing figures which would *not* be touched.

For instance, when New York Central was 131 he predicted that it would sell at 145 before 129.

So repeatedly did his figures prove to be accurate, and so different did his work appear from that of any expert whose methods we had examined, that we set about to investigate Mr. Gann and his way of figuring out these predictions, as well as the particular use which he was making of them in the market.

The results of this investigation are remarkable in many ways.

It appears to be a fact that Mr. Gann has developed an entirely new idea as to the principles governing stock market movements. He bases his operations upon certain natural laws which, though existing since the world began, have only in recent years been subjected to the will of man, and added to the list of so-called modern discoveries.

We have asked Mr. Gann for an outline of his work, and have secured some remarkable evidence as to the results obtained therefrom. We submit this in full recognition of the fact that in Wall Street a man with a new idea—an idea which violates the traditions and encourages a scientific view of the proposition—is not usually welcomed by the majority, for the reason that he stimulates thought and research. These activities said majority abhors.

Mr. Gann's description of his experience and methods is given herewith. It should be read with a recognition of the established fact that Mr. Gann's predictions have proved correct in a large majority of instances.

"For the past ten years I have devoted my entire time and attention to the speculative markets. Like many others,

I lost thousands of dollars and experienced the usual ups and downs incidental to the novice who enters the market without preparatory knowledge of the subject.

"I soon began to realize that all successful men, whether lawyers, doctors, or scientists, devoted years of time to the study and investigation of their particular pursuit or profession before attempting to make any money out of it.

"Being in the brokerage business myself and handling large accounts, I had opportunities seldom afforded the ordinary man for studying the cause of success and failure in the speculations of others. I found that over ninety per cent of the traders who go into the market without knowledge or study usually lose in the end.

"I soon began to note the periodical recurrence of the rise and fall in stocks and commodities. This led me to conclude that natural law was the basis of market movements. I then decided to devote ten years of my life to the study of natural law as applicable to the speculative markets and to devote my best energies toward making speculation a profitable profession. After exhaustive researches and investigations of the known sciences, I discovered that the Law of Vibration enabled me to accurately determine the exact points to which stocks or commodities should rise and fall within a given time. The working out of this law determines the cause and predicts the effect long before the Street is aware of either. Most speculators can testify to the fact that it is looking at the effect and ignoring the cause that has produced their losses.

"It is impossible here to give an adequate idea of the Law of Vibration as I apply it to the markets, however, the layman may be able to grasp some of the principles when I state that the Law of Vibration is the fundamental law upon which wireless telegraphy, wireless telephones and phonographs are based. Without the existence of this law the above inventions would have been impossible.

"In order to test out the efficiency of my idea I have not only put in years of labor in the regular way, but I spent nine months working night and day in the Astor Library of New York and in the British Museum of London, going over the records of stock transactions as far back as 1820. I have incidentally examined the manipulations of Jay Gould. Daniel Drew, Commodore Vanderbilt, and all the other important Wall Street manipulators from that time to the present day. I have examined every quotation of Union Pacific prior to and from the time of E. H. Harriman's securing control, and can say that of all the manipulations in the history of Wall Street, Mr. Harriman's was the most masterly. The figures show that, whether unconsciously or not, Mr. Harriman worked strictly in accordance with natural law.

"In going over the history of markets and the great mass of related statistics, it soon becomes apparent that certain laws govern the changes and variations in the value of stocks and there exists a periodic or cyclic law, which is at the back of all these movements. Observation has shown that there are regular periods of intense activity on the Exchange followed by periods of inactivity. Mr. Henry Hall, in his recent book devoted much space to 'Cycles of Prosperity and Depression' which he found recurring at regular intervals of time. The law which I have applied will not only give these long cycles or swings, but the daily and even hourly movements of stocks. By knowing the exact vibration of each individual stock I am able to determine at what point each will receive support and at what point the greatest resistance is to be met.

"Those in close touch with the markets have noticed the phenomena of ebb and flow, or rise and fall in the value of stocks. At certain times a stock will become intensely active, large transactions being made in it; at other times this same stock will become practically stationary or inactive with a very small volume of sales. I have found that the Law of Vibration governs and controls these conditions. I have also found that certain phases of this law govern the rise in a stock and an entirely different rule operates on the decline.

"While Union Pacific and other railroad stocks which made their high prices in August were declining, United States

Steel common was steadily advancing. The Law of Vibration was at work, sending a particular stock on the upward trend, whilst others were trending downward.

"I have found that in the stock itself exists its harmonic or inharmonic relationship to the driving power or force behind it. The secret of all its activity is therefore apparent. By my method I can determine the vibration of each stock and by also taking certain time values into consideration I can in the majority of cases tell exactly what the stock will do under given conditions.

"The power to determine the trend of the market is due to my knowledge of the characteristics of each individual stock and a certain grouping of different stocks under their proper rates of vibration. Stocks are like electrons, atoms, and molecules, which hold persistently to their own individuality in response to the fundamental Law of Vibration. Science teaches 'that an original impulse of any kind finally resolves itself into periodic or rythmical motion,' also 'just as the pendulum returns again in its swing, just as the moon returns in its orbit, just as the advancing year ever brings the rose of spring, so do the properties of the elements periodically recur as the weight of the atoms rises.'

"From my extensive investigations, studies and applied tests, I find that not only do the various stocks vibrate, but that the driving forces controlling the stocks are also in a state of vibration. These vibratory forces can only be known by the movements they generate on the stocks and their values in the market. Since all great swings or movements of the market are cyclic they act in accordance with periodic law.

"Science has laid down the principle that 'the propertities of an element are a periodic function of its atomic weight.' A famous scientist has stated that 'we are brought to the conviction that diversity in phenomenal nature in its different kingdoms, is most intimately associated with numerical relationship. The numbers are not intermixed, chaotically and accidentally, but are subject to regular periodicity. The changes and developments are also seen to be in many cases undulatory.'

"Thus, I affirm, every class of phenomena, whether in nature or in the stock market, must be subject to the universal law of causation and harmony. Every effect must have an adequate cause.

"If we wish to avert failure in speculation we must deal with causes. Everything in existence is based on exact proportion and perfect relationship. There is no chance in nature, because mathematical principles of the highest order lie at the foundation of all things. Faraday said: 'There is nothing in the Universe but mathematical points of force.'

"Vibration is fundamental; nothing is exempt from this law; it is universal, therefore applicable to every class of phenomena on the globe.

"Through the Law of Vibration every stock in the market moves in its own distinctive sphere of activities, as to intensity, volume and direction; all the essential qualities of its evolution are characterized in its own rate of vibration. Stocks, like atoms, are really centers of energies, therefore they are controlled mathematically. Stocks create their own field of action and power; power to attract and repel, which principle explains why certain stocks at times lead the market and 'turn dead' at other times. Thus to speculate scientifically it is absolutely necessary to follow natural law.

"After years of patient study I have proven to my entire satisfaction as well as demonstrated to others that vibration explains every possible phase and condition of the market."

In order to substantiate Mr. Gann's claims as to what he has been able to do under this method, we called upon Mr. William E. Gilley, an Inspector of Imports, 16 Beaver street, New York. Mr. Gilley is well-known in the down-town district. He himself has studied stock market movements for twenty-five years, during which time he has examined every piece of market literature that has been issued and procurable in Wall Street. It was he who encouraged Mr. Gann to study out the scientific and mathematical possibilities of the subject. When asked what had been the most impressive of Mr. Gann's work and predictions, he replied as follows:

"It is very difficult for me to remember all the predictions and operations of

Mr. Gann which may be classed as phenomenal, but the following are a few: In 1908 when Union Pacific was 168⅛, he told me that it would not touch 169 before it had a good break. We sold it short all the way down to 152⅝, covering on the weak spots and putting it out again on the rallies, securing twenty-three points profit out of an eighteen-point move.

"He came to me when United States Steel was selling around 50 and said 'This Steel will run up to 58 but it will not sell at 59. From there it should break 16¾ points.' We sold it short around 58⅜ with a stop at 59. The highest it went was 58¾. From there it declined to 41¼—17½ points.

"At another time wheat was selling at about 89c. He predicted that the May option would sell at $1.35. We bought it and made large profits on the way up. It actually touched $1.35½.

"When Union Pacific was 172, he said it would go to 184⅞ but not an eighth higher until it had had a good break. It went to 184⅞ and came back from there eight or nine times. We sold it short repeatedly with a stop at 185 and were never caught. It eventually came back to 172½.

"Mr. Gann's calculations are based on natural law. I have followed his work closely for years. I know that he has a firm grasp of the basic principles which govern stock market movements, and I do not believe any other man on earth can duplicate the idea or his method at the present time.

"Early this year he figured that the top of the advance would fall on a certain day in August and calculated the prices at which the Dow-Jones averages would then stand. The market culminated on the exact day and within four-tenths of one per cent. of the figures predicted."

"You and Mr. Gann must have cleaned up considerable money on all these operations," was suggested.

"Yes, we have made a great deal of money. He has taken half a million dollars out of the market in the past few years. I once saw him take $130, and in less than one month run it up to over $12,000. He can compound money faster than any man I ever met."

"One of the most astonishing calculations made by Mr. Gann was during last summer (1909) when he predicted that September wheat would sell at $1.20. This meant that it must touch that figure before the end of the month of September. At twelve o'clock, Chicago time, on September 30th (the last day) the option was selling below $1.08, and it looked as though his prediction would not be fulfilled. Mr. Gann said 'If it does not touch $1.20 by the close of the market it will prove that there is something wrong with my whole method of calculation. I do not care what the price is now, it must go there.' It is common history that September wheat surprised the whole country by selling at $1.20 and no higher in the very last hour of the trading, closing at that figure."

So much for what Mr. Gann has said and done as evidenced by himself and others. Now as to what demonstrations have taken place before our representative:

During the month of October, 1909, in twenty-five market days, Mr. Gann made, in the presence of our representative, two hundred and eighty-six transactions in various stocks, on both the long and short side of the market. Two hundred and sixty-four of these transactions resulted in profits; twenty-two in losses.

The capital with which he operated was doubled ten times, so that at the end of the month he had one thousand per cent. on his original margin.

In our presence Mr. Gann sold Steel common short at 94⅞, saying that it would not go to 95. It did not.

On a drive which occurred during the week ending October 29th, Mr. Gann bought Steel common at 86¼, saying that it would not go to 86. The lowest it sold was 86⅛.

We have seen him give in one day sixteen successive orders in the same stock, eight of which turned out to be at either the top or the bottom eighth of that particular swing. The above we can positively verify.

Such performances as these, coupled with the foregoing, are probably unparalleled in the history of the Street.

James R. Keene has said, "The man who is right six times out of ten will make his fortune." Here is a trader, who, without any attempt to make a showing (for he did not know the results were to be published), establishes a record of over ninety-two per cent profitable trades.

Mr. Gann has refused to disclose his method at any price, but to those scientifically inclined he has unquestionably added to the stock of Wall Street knowledge and pointed out infinite possibilities.

We have requested Mr. Gann to figure out for the readers of THE TICKER a few of the most striking indications which appear in his calculations. In presenting these we wish it understood that no man, in or out of Wall Street, is infallible.

Mr. Gann's figures at present indicate that the trend of the stock market should, barring the usual rallies, be toward lower prices until March or April, 1910.

He calculates that May wheat, which is now selling at $1.02, should not sell below 99c. and should sell at $1.45 next spring.

On cotton, which is now at about the 15c. level, he estimates that, after a good reaction from these prices, the commodity should reach 18c. in the spring of 1910. He looks for a corner in the March or May option.

Whether these figures prove correct or not, will in no sense detract from the record which Mr. Gann has already established.

Mr. Gann was born in Lufkin, Texas, and is thirty-one years of age. He is a gifted mathematician, has an extraordinary memory for figures, and is an expert Tape Reader. Take away his science and he would beat the market on his intuitive tape reading alone.

Endowed as he is with such qualities, we have no hesitation in predicting that within a comparatively few years Wm. D. Gann will receive full recognition as one of Wall Street's leading operators.

R. D. W.

NOTE:—Since the above forecast was made, Cotton has suffered the expected decline, the extreme break having been 120 points. The lowest on May wheat thus far has been $1.01⅜. It is now selling at $1.06¼.

Bird's Eye Views

Studies of Value Based on a Broad Survey of Conditions That Make Prices

By G. C. SELDEN

III. The Rock Island Company and the Great Southwest

THE story of the Rock Island Company in recent years is the story of the Southwest. It is the great rush of population into Kansas, Oklahoma and Texas, the development of "dry farming," the opening up of Indian lands and the diversification of both crops and industries, which have been the mainstay of that enormous network of railways now included in the Rock Island holding company.

It is equally true that the Rock Island Company has helped to bring about these conditions. More than any other railway, probably, Rock Island has been the "friend of the farmer." By extensive advertising, by low-rate home-seekers' excursions, and by pushing its tracks aggressively across the vacant prairies, the Rock Island management has done much to hasten the development of its territory.

A RAILROAD EMPIRE

The Rock Island System lies in seventeen states. It reaches Minneapolis and South Dakota on the north, Galveston and New Orleans in the south; Chicago, Evansville and Birmingham on the east, Denver, Pueblo and New Mexico on the west.

All this vast region is a rapidly growing and prosperous territory, but it is in the Southwest especially that nature is overturning her cornucopia on the heads of the wind-swept farmers. The following table shows the growth of population in the Southwest as estimated by the United States Census Department:

Growth of Population in the Southwest

	1900	1909
Missouri	3,107,000	3,491,000
Arkansas	1,312,000	1,477,000
Kansas	1,471,000	1,707,000
Oklahoma	790,000	1,592,000
Texas	3,049,000	3,781,000
Colorado	540,000	654,000
New Mexico	195,000	227,000

In these seven states the total railroad mileage of all companies increased from

enterprises are being undertaken every day, farmers are raising new crops, new land is being brought under cultivation.

During the last fiscal year 402 new industries were established along the tracks of the C. R. I. & P. Ry., estimated to create a movement of over 57,000 carloads annually; on the "Frisco Lines" (a part of the Rock Island Co.) were established 327 industries, estimated to load in and out over 80,000 carloads annually.

Recent reports are that the trains in the Southwest are carrying more passengers than ever before. Pullman sleeping cars are crowded, extra trains are running on nearly every line. Gross earnings of the entire Rock Island System (including the 'Frisco) for 1908-9

A STEAM PLOUGH IN OKLAHOMA—21 FURROWS

34,000 in 1898 to 45,000 in 1908—or 30.5 per cent; total freight traffic increased 90 per cent.; total passenger traffic about 170 per cent.—and yet 1908 was the panic year. Freight traffic in 1908 fell off about 2,700,000 tons from 1907, but 1909 seems likely to exceed 1907.

It is doubtful if this record was ever before equaled in this country or elsewhere. An increase of 90 per cent. in freight traffic and 170 per cent. in passenger traffic for a stretch of territory covering seven states (one of which is Texas—Have you ever traveled across Texas?) in ten years is, as the office boy says, "the limit."

NEW INDUSTRIES

Moreover, it looks as though the Southwest had only begun to grow. New

fell only a few thousand dollars short of the banner year 1906-7, in spite of the small business during the first half of the year 1908-9. Earnings since the close of the year have been advancing rapidly and there is no question that the Rock Island Company is now doing far the largest business in its history.

Settlers have only scratched the surface of possibilities in the great Southwest. Texans, in that modest, unassuming way of theirs, say that their state can raise anything that any other state can grow, raise more of it, and of a better quality. At some points along the coast land is selling for $500 or $1,000 an acre, for agricultural purposes alone. The stories of truck gardening, Bermuda onions, magnolia figs, satsuma oranges, peaches (both the edible and the dimpled varieties), alfalfa-grown hogs, blooded stock, petroleum, the mines of El Paso—not to mention such commonplace articles as wheat, corn and cotton, are enough to make the poor benighted non-Texan hide his diminished head in shame.

The roads that connect the great centers of the Mississippi basin—Chicago, St. Louis, Kansas City, Minneapolis, Omaha, Des Moines, Memphis, Birmingham, New Orleans—with the new Southwest empire, are assured of a great future.

And Mexico must not be overlooked. A big development of the mining industry and a gradual increase in agriculture are in sight for the junior republic and the resulting interchange of traffic with

The result of this "wheels within wheels" arrangement is a sort of pyramid of numerous stocks and bonds of subsidiary companies, at the top of which is found the Rock Island holding company, with only $49,000,000 preferred stock and $90,000,000 common stock outstanding, but controlling 14,553 miles of road. This figures out about $3,400 of preferred stock and $6,200 of common stock per mile, compared with $27,000 of stock per mile for the Atchison System, for example.

Each of the successive companies, on the way up, pays its dividends from the profits of its subsidiaries. These profits keep piling up as you go up the scale of companies, like the tide driven into

CUTTING ALFALFA IN TEXAS—FIFTH CROP OF THE SEASON.

the Missippi basin will be important.

ORGANIZATION OF ROCK ISLAND CO.

The Rock Island Company is a holding company and owns practically the entire stock of the Chicago, Rock Island and Pacific Railroad Company. This latter company owns nearly all the stock of the Chicago, Rock Island and Pacific Railway Co., called "Rock Island Lines," and nearly all the common stock of the St. Louis and San Francisco Co., commonly called " 'Frisco Lines." Both Rock Island Lines and the 'Frisco Lines are operating companies and also own interests in various subsidiary companies. One of the companies owned by the 'Frisco Lines is the important Chicago and Eastern Illinois Railroad, which in turn owns the Evansville and Terre Haute Railroad.

the spreading mouth of a river. This cumulative movement of profits is what has sent Rock Island Co. to near the top of THE TICKER's "Bargain Indicator" in a few months.

MARGIN OF SAFETY

Not only is the capital stock of the holding company very small in proportion to the extent of the enterprise, but the "margin of safety," or percentage of net income remaining after payment of all fixed charges, is exceeding narrow. In 1908 the margin of safety for the Rock Island Co. as a whole was only 4.3 per cent compared with 48 per cent. for the Atchison system, 60 per cent. for St. Paul, 19 per cent. for Missouri Pacific, etc. It will be seen that a deficit was narrowly escaped. For 1909 the margin of safety rose to 11.2 per cent.—

still relatively small; for 1907 it was 25 per cent.

Suppose you had an air-tight engine boiler with an open standpipe in the top of it. The water would rise slowly in the boiler, but as soon as the boiler was full the water would go up very fast in the standpipe; likewise when you started to draw off the water, it would go down very fast in the standpipe.

The boiler represents the fixed charges and the standpipe represents the amount applicable to dividends on the stock. A moderate change in earnings produces a big change in the amount applicable to dividends.

Here are two conditions which tend to make Rock Island dividends fluctuate: (1) Small capital stock; (2) Small margin of safety; or, heavy fixed charges in proportion to net earnings.

DEVELOPMENT OF ROCK ISLAND SYSTEM

When this big holding company was organized in 1902, it might have been concisely described as a loosely connected aggregation of second-grade railroads, heavily overweighted with fixed charges.

The capitalization of future earnings was quite as striking in Rock Island as in the United States Steel Corporation, but in each instance the growth of the business and the development of the country have apparently been sufficient to pull the company through.

Results obtained by the Rock Island Lines within the last fiscal year were especially notable. Although gross earnings increased $2,700,000, transportation expenses were $750,000 less than the previous year. This decrease in operating costs was not obtained by failure to maintain way and structures in good condition, for the cost of maintenance of both the road and equipment showed an increase. Mileage of 85 pound rails was increased, as was also stone-ballasted mileage. Several timber bridges were replaced with steel and a number of bridges and trestles were filled in.

Automatic block signals have been installed on 346 miles of road and the telephone system of train dispatching has been put in on 420 miles.

SPECULATIVE POSSIBILITIES

It is clear from the above analysis that the stocks of the Rock Island Co. have great speculative possibilities. With continued prosperity in the West and Southwest, and with no untoward accident to interrupt the progress of the country, net earnings will show great increases.

A large part of these earnings should go back into the property in the way of improvements and extensions. The annual report of Rock Island Lines shows $2,600,000 applied to additions and betterments during the year, and if that road and the 'Frisco are to be brought up to the standard of Atchison and St. Paul such expenditures must continue. Even after allowing for this, however, a substantial surplus should be left for dividends on the preferred, and eventually on the common.

On the other hand, another panic like that which laid Texas flat on its back in 1908 might result in sending the Rock Island Co. to the pawnbroker.

Rock Island stocks are not as yet in the investment class, but they are likely to become speculative favorites. The public prefers to trade in stocks selling under or around par. People hesitate to buy a stock at 200 or over, not only because it looks high but because of heavy interest charges on margin accounts. When public buying gets started in a stock like Rock Island common, no one knows where it will end.

Rock Island preferred has an advantage in that it is entitled by the charter to increasing dividends as time passes— 4 per cent. in 1909, 5 per cent. 1910 to 1916, and 6 per cent. in 1917 and thereafter.

So long as the country is prosperous, the Rock Island issues will be safe to hold and there is hardly a stock on the list with more attractive speculative possibilities. When the next panic begins to cast its shadows before, holders of the stock will do well to make a critical examination of both the financial and physical condition of the property at that time.

Studies in Stock Speculation

Designed Especially for Those Who Cannot Attend Their Brokers' Offices

By ROLLO TAPE

Author of "Studies in Tape Reading"

II. How to Determine the Trend

TO select and adhere to a definite plan of operation is the most important factor in any kind of enterprise. This is doubly true in stock market affairs. Here the man who works methodically is actually helped by the hordes of people who wobble about the Street, catching at straws, recklessly venturing their capital on promiscuous ideas.

But before one is equipped to select the plan best suited to his purse and his individual characteristics, he must know and examine methods of every description. We will therefore briefly outline the different ways of money making which may be adopted by traders who are distant a few blocks to a few thousand miles from Wall Streeet.

METHOD NO. 1:—PLAYING PANICS. This is probably the simplest, safest and surest of stock market methods. Panics have occurred in recent years as follows: 1890, 1893, 1895, 1901, 1903, 1905, 1907; viz., seven panics in nineteen years, or an average of one every two years and eight months. Stocks bought outright at such times and held for the boom which invariably follows, will generally show from 50 to 100% increase in market value.

To buy in a panic requires cash and courage. Every one knows when a panic exists, and the more experience one has, the better he can judge when the actual bottom is reached. Knowing which stocks to buy requires further knowledge, but The Bargain Indicator which appears monthly in THE TICKER shows which issues are selling at the lowest prices on the basis of value. In a general way the time to sell is also easily recognized, but no one can hope to pick the exact top.

This entire operation requires a great deal of patience. It can frequently be followed successfully by those who know least about speculation. If stocks are rightly bought and fully paid for under this plan, losses are unnecessary. When the operator's holdings have been liquidated, the most approved method requires the proceeds to be placed in a trust company, where interest will be drawn until the next panic.

METHOD NO. 2:—TRADING FOR THE TWENTY-POINT SWINGS. This requires knowledge of values, of the trend and other technical points, as will be explained later on. These opportunities occur in the leading stocks two or three times a year. The trader can operate on the long side, buying for cash only, or he can deal on margin, taking either the long or short side and using stop orders. Frequent small losses must be taken.

METHOD NO. 3:—TRADING FOR THE FIVE- AND TEN-POINT SWINGS. This is about as close a method as can well be used by one who does not follow the ticker daily. Anything under five points in the active stocks would seem to be within the realm of scalping, or of tape reading.*

This method calls for a two-point stop

---

*In these classifications the swings of leading stocks, such as Union, Reading and Steel, are the basis; the others as a rule fluctuate less widely and in proportion to their price.

on the majority of trades and as trading is more frequent and active, losses are more numerous. The object is to make profits exceed losses. Closer study of the market is necessary, as chances to trade may occur from one to several times a week.

METHOD NO. 4:—MECHANICAL TRADING. This is one of the oldest methods. Thousands of people have followed the mechanical idea but only one man has publicly established the fact that he is able to show average profits in all kinds of markets. His knowledge of the subject—his plan—cannot be published. But there are many recognized mechanical helps which, as we will show, can be used in connection with the other plans.

We cannot set forth any purely mechanical method of trading; all such which have heretofore been advocated by their many followers having failed in the final test, the one mentioned being the sole exception.

METHOD NO. 5:—ARBITRAGING ON RIGHTS, ETC. This style of operating requires knowledge of corporate as well as stock market affairs. It consists of figuring the value of rights as compared to value of stocks into which they are convertible or exchangable. Having figured a profit, the operator buys the rights and simultaneously goes short of the equivalent in new securities, the latter to be delivered when issued by the company. As soon as this time arrives, the exchange is made, the new securities delivered, thus completing the transaction. The broker handles all details. To carry on these operations one must be an expert at figures. On the surface there is little risk, but unforeseen delays or legal complications frequently turn profits into losses.

METHOD NO. 6:—TRADING AGAINST CONVERTIBLE BONDS. This plan enables one to sell short a stock which is convertible into bonds, going long of the bonds at the same time. This can be done to advantage when a severe decline is anticipated, the basis of the idea being that the stock will decline more than the bonds. There is a minimum of risk in this way of trading.

METHOD NO. 7:—TRADING ON INITIAL ACTIVITY OF A STOCK. This requires one to keep a careful record of daily move-

ments and volumes, in practically the whole list of stocks. This method can be followed scientifically and with limited risk.

METHOD NO. 8:—TRADING ON "THE TICKER'S" BARGAIN INDICATOR. We suggest this in a tentative way. Past records show that money could have been made thus, and the letters of numerous subscribers indicate that good results have thus been obtained. These will be fully discussed.

METHOD NO. 9:—BUYING BANKRUPT STOCKS. Many fortunes have been made by those who have purchased securities of properties undergoing receivership. There is an approved way of carrying out this idea, and one that, in these days of expanding railroad traffic, can scarcely ever fail to show profits.

METHOD. NO. 10:—SELLING SHORT WHEN RIGHTS ARE ANNOUNCED. This to some may seem precarious, but there is a time and a way that it can be done advantageously.

METHOD NO. 11:—TRADING ON LONDON PRIVILEGES. This necessitates an original outlay for the Put or Call instead of margin being deposited. There are many ways of ultilizing these privileges. The risk is limited to the cost of the privilege.

Here we have stated eleven different methods of trading, all more or less scientific in nature, and available to the needs of traders who cannot attend their brokers' offices. No consideration has been given to trading on so-called "Information" as a large majority of all tips go wrong, and the idea of trading on what another person says or thinks is about as illogical as anything can well be.

We have also disregarded all schemes based on scale buying or selling, experience having shown that those who operate on this principle usually encounter a period where their capital or their nerve, or both, become exhausted. This of course refers to margin trading. It does not apply if a person buys outright when prices are low and holds until they recover.

We will exclude also the popular fallacy which moves people to buy stocks just before the dividends come off.

The object here is to consider only such plans as permit of scientific analysis and logical solution; wherein certain effects are due to specified causes.

As to which plan will show the best results, this depends upon the individual. Certain methods require more capital, others more nerve, patience, study, etc. After going into the merits of each, the trader can decide for himself which he prefers to employ.

Frequently more than one plan can be operated simultaneously, or two or three will confirm each other.

TECHNICAL KNOWLEDGE REQUIRED

Of course it would be of some advantage if we were to begin with the A B C of the stock market and explain each little point as we go along. Were we certain that the majority of our readers were novices there would be strong reason for this. But as a very great proportion are highly experienced in the business of speculation and the balance are more or less so, too much attention

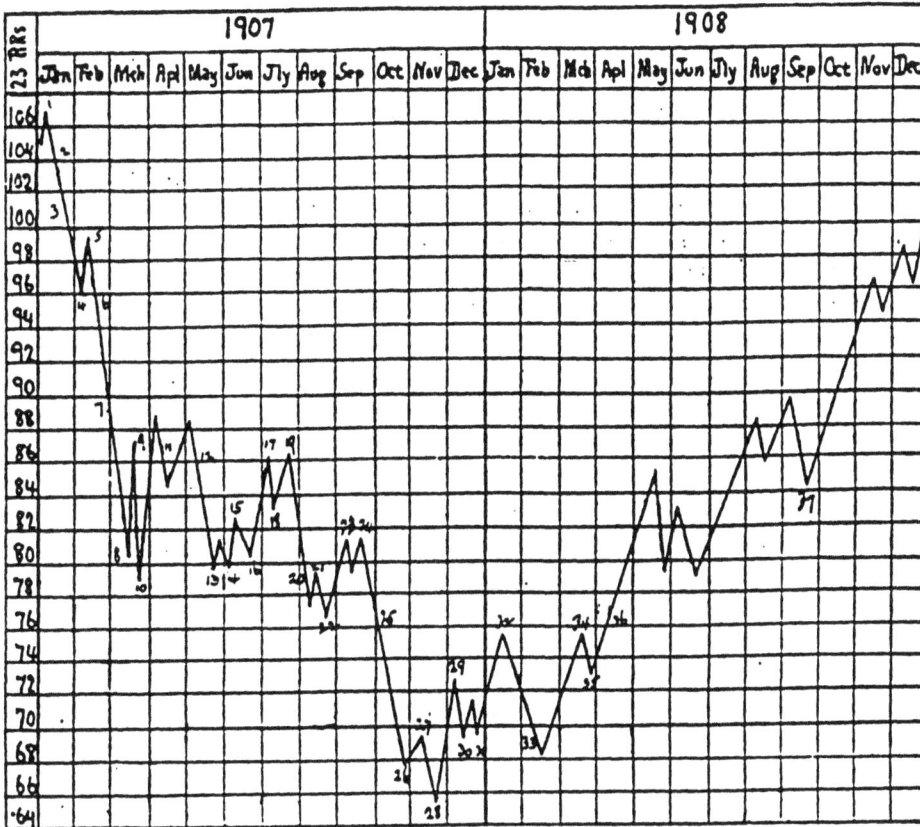

Movements of twenty-three Active Railroad Stocks,
1907 and 1908. Gibson's Averages. Moves of less than
two points disregarded.

to elementary points would be burdensome. So let those to whom the simpler points are not clear, consult the four preceding bound volumes of THE TICKER. There will be found explanations of practically every point which is likely to puzzle them. The idea is that a student should know how to read and spell before taking up history or geography.

KNOWING THE TREND

There are certain factors which should be clearly recognized by all, no matter which plan it is decided to adopt. The most important is knowing the trend.

It is better to be able to correctly judge the trend than to know which stocks to buy or sell.

A trader may select the most promising stock—be absolutely right in his decision—yet if he does not act in accordance with the trend, he will usually buy or sell at the time his losses are apt to be numerous.

On the other hand, if a person can correctly distinguish this trend and uses it as his sole guide, he can make money without knowing a thing about earnings, values, dividends or prospects.

The trend, therefore, requires our careful study and consideration. Let us investigate the subject and see what we can learn.

A bull market is one in which demand exceeds supply. This is evidenced by rising prices. New high levels are frequently made, the general up trend being interrupted occasionally by declines due to technical conditions and accidents. A bear market is the reverse.

By drawing a chart we form a picture of what a market has done, so let us take a chart of the bear market of 1907 and the bull market of 1908, and, in order to study it, number and examine the points of interest.

(1) The month starts with an up trend which quickly turns down.

(2) The line goes below the opening figure. If the opening were a bottom this would show weakness.

(3) Down trend clearly defined.

(4) At this level, resistance is encountered. (Remember that as this chart records no moves of less than two points, at least a two-point "turn up" must take place before this resistance point can be formed.)

(5) The line continues to rise to about 99½. As it once more turns down and approaches 96, we watch to see whether the support at that level is still effective. If 96 is broken through, we shall understand that the trend is still down.

(6) There is no support whatever at this figure. The line goes plunging through.

(7) The month closes with the trend still pointing downward.

(8) First resistance after a decline of nearly twenty points, and as we all remember this marked the first bottom made during the 1907 panic.

(9) Here we have the extreme of the first rally after the panic and as history shows that, following a panic, stocks usually recede to the low point before starting on the permanent recovery, we expect the line to again touch the 80 mark.

(10) The decline extends to about 79. This is a trifle below the previous bottom, and at any other time than just after a panic would mean still lower prices. But panics do not follow each other so closely, so we decide that the trend from around this level should be up. It being a recognized fact that a normal rally is one-half the decline, we figure (without regarding any movements prior to those shown here), that prices having declined from 107 to 79 —28 points—there should be a rally of about 14 points. This would bring the line up to 93. If the rally of one-half is accomplished it can be regarded as a fair indication that the lowest prices have been seen for the present. If not, we must be on the look-out for a further decline.

(11) The rally only extends to 89, followed by a reaction to 84½. This does not look very bullish, considering that the top of this rally is only slightly higher than the previous one. Perhaps the third rally will go higher. At least it should if the rise is to continue.

NOTE:—A rising trend is simply one in which the demand for stocks is constantly overcoming the supply. When this increasing demand falls off it is instantly reflected in the price. So in our reasonings as to what the market should do, we are merely making forecasts based on the facts in hand relating to this supply and demand. We also judge as much by what the market fails to do as by what it does.

(12) When the line comes back to this point (about 86½) we know that the third top not only failed to go higher, but fell slightly short of the one preceding. This indicates that the supply of stocks at this level has overcome the demand. In Street parlance, "stocks are for sale on rallies." It is a critical point, and the next move above 88½ or below 84½ should decide the direction of the

immediate swing. At the moment the balance is in favor of prices again declining, but we should not yet decide that the trend had definitely turned downward. The price finally breaks through and at 84 we know it is going lower. If the market does not now meet support at the panic levels, followed by a normal rally to 93, we shall have evidence that the worst has not yet been seen.

(13) At this point there is sufficient demand to produce a feeble rally.

(14) The rally does not hold, but buyers are strong enough to again turn the course upward.

(15) This time the top is a little higher than before and

(16) This turning point is a little higher than the two previous bottoms. The subsequent rise gives us a higher top.

(17) This rally offers some encouragement to the bulls, in view of the formation below it.

(18) Support is higher than the bottom marked 16 and now if the market is to go on advancing the next rally should carry the line well above point 17.

(19) But the rally halts at the same level as before, showing the market devoid of lifting power, and that pressure still exists. Note that tops marked 17 and 19 are lower than those preceding Nos. 11 and 12. This indicates a diminution of strength, and is in itself a sign of lower prices.

Now we have the line, in a sense, penned in between the levels of 18 and 19. Whichever way the market goes out of this field will give us a pretty clear idea of the trend.

Prices break below the bottom marked 18. This is a very bearish indication, as it shows that rallies do not hold. The decline continues steadily and at the 80 line (the panic level) there is no support.

(20) Here we have strong confirmation that the trend is down.

(21) A weak rally.

(22) A still lower range.

(23-4) More weak rallies. Tops lower than 17 and 19.

(25) No support at the previous turn.

(26) After such a tremendous decline we must look for a sharp rally; but it does not come. We know that panic prevails and that bull markets begin in panics, so we look out for the change in trend which should develop after the rally.

(27) The rally is slight, showing that the pressure is still on.

(28) When this point is reached there is chaos in the Street, and we recognize that while it is possible for prices to go still lower, they are bound to turn up from somewhere about this level—temporarily, at least.

(29) This is a fair rally. Let us see what follows.

(30) A comparatively small reaction. Support is higher up. The rally which follows is valuable. It fences the market in and after another bottom (31) is made the line forges through to a new high level (32) representing a substantial recovery and confirming the up trend.

(33) The decline to this level puts us temporarily in doubt as to whether or not the trend has again turned down.

(34) Here the advance is disputed again at the same level as 32 but the small reaction (35) and the subsequent reaching up above into a higher field (36) reassures us that the bulls are in control.

From this time on until the end of the year the up trend is only once in doubt, when the bottom (37) is made a couple of points lower than the one preceding. Here we hesitate until the line again rises above 90, after which the "steps up" are unbroken.

The above will give an idea as to how the trend may be read from the market itself.

I find that if we have a clear understanding of the basic principles of stock market movements, we recognize them in the long swings, the short swings, the daily and even the half hourly movements of the market and of individual stocks.

The above principle in all cases is the same—supply and demand. When demand exceeds supply we find the supporting points (points of resistance, as I have previously designated them) higher and higher. When supply predominates we get lowering levels of support and pressure. When supply and demand are equalized we have a lifeless market.

A study of the trend, therefore, is a study of supply and demand—pressure and support.

Identically the same indications as have been shown here are found in the minor movements of the market or of any one stock as prices come out on the ticker tape. (See "Studies in Tape Reading"*). If these small swings are remembered or recorded, it will be seen at once that they correspond to the larger movements. This may be demonstrated by anyone who will make separate charts showing every one-eighth movement of a single stock, or every one point, two point or five point movement; also, by making a composite chart of three, ten or twenty leading stocks, or groups of railroad, industrial, equipment or mining stocks.

The principal difficulty lies in the interpretation of the movements. This is something which a person can only acquire by practice. Experiments with various kinds of charts and records will enable one to decide from which he can obtain the best results.

In judging the trend of the whole market, however, it will not do to take one or two stocks, or even a small group of stocks. The more issues included the greater the accuracy of the forecast.

The best known "Average Prices" are those compiled by Dow, Jones & Co., and published in *The Wall Street Journal*. These are based on the prices of the following twenty railroad stocks:

Atchison, Brooklyn Rapid Transit, Canadian Pacific, Delaware & Hudson, Northwestern, St. Paul, Twin City Rapid Transit, Erie, Louisville & Nashville, Northern Pacific, Missouri Pacific, New York Central, Pennsylvania, Reading, Southern Pacific, Southern Railway, Union Pacific, Norfolk & Western, Baltimore & Ohio and Illinois Central; and twelve industrial stocks: viz.,

Smelters, Amalgamated Copper, United States Rubber common and preferred, National Lead, United States Steel common and preferred, Peoples Gas, Sugar common, General Electric,

*Ticker Pub. Co., N. Y., $3.10 postpaid.

Colorado Fuel & Iron and American Car & Foundry.

In arriving at these averages Dow, Jones & Co. take the *bid* prices at the close of each day's session. Now it is obvious that between one day's close and the next there may occur very wide swings; therefore, under this method of calculating, the real tops and bottoms for the day are completely lost.

The same is true of Thomas Gibson's average prices. These are made up of twenty-three active rails and eighteen active industrials. Mr. Gibson considers the last sale of each stock, and if there is no sale for the day, he takes the figure half way between the closing bid and asked price. The following stocks are used in compiling the Gibson averages:

Rails: Atchison, Baltimore & Ohio, Canadian Pacific, Chesapeake & Ohio, Colorado & Southern, Denver & Rio Grande, Erie, Illinois Central, Louis. & Nash., Missouri, Kansas & Texas, Missouri Pacific, N. Y. Central, Norfolk & Western, Northern Pacific, Pennsylvania, Reading, Rock Island, Southern Pacific, Southern Railway, Union Pacific, Wabash.

Industrials: Amalgamated Copper, American Car & Foundry, American Locomotive, American Smelting & Refining, American Sugar, Anaconda, Colorado Fuel & Iron, Corn Products, Distillers' Securities, General Electric, National Lead, People's Gas, Pressed Steel Car, Republic Iron & Steel, Consolidated Gas, U. S. Realty & Improvement, U. S. Steel com., U. S. Steel pfd.

HOW TO FORM A TREND INDICATOR.

It seems to me that a more reliable trend indicator than either of the above may be made by forming a chart showing the average daily highest, lowest and mean price of ten leading railroad and ten leading industrial stocks, this mean price forming the real trend indicator. This eliminates all the extreme moves and gives one a steady and well balanced compass. The stocks which appear the best for this purpose, together with the easiest way of compiling them, will be found below.

Take the summary of transactions as printed in your newspaper; set down for each the highest and the lowest figures touched on that day, as though it were the cost of 100 full shares at that price. That is, instead of 203⅝ for Union Pacific, put down $20,362.50, etc. We suggest this because it is easier for most people to add and divide figures than fractions.

When completed the day's table should appear as follows:

How to Form a Trend Indicator

RAILROAD STOCKS.	HIGHEST.	LOWEST.
1 Union Pacific	20,362.50	20,175.
2 Reading	16,325.	16,175.
3 St. Paul	15,850.	15,750.
4 Atchison	12,025.	11,912.50
5 Southern Pacific	13,075	12,937.50
6 Pennsylvania	14,237.50	14,150.
7 Northern Pacific	14,875.	14,800.
8 New York Central	13,437.50	13,362.50
9 Chesapeake & Ohio	8,850.	8,775.
10 Missouri Pacific	7,025.	6,987.
INDUSTRIAL STOCKS.		
1 U. S. Steel com.	9,162.50	9,037.50
2 Amalgamated Copper	8,762.50	8,625.
3 Smelters	9,887.50	9,787.50
4 Car Foundry	7,550.	7,450.
5 Locomotive	6,250.	6,200.
6 Am. Agri. Chemical	4,900.	4,900.
7 Colorado Fuel	5,037.50	4,912.50
8 Nat. Lead	8,900.	8,837.50
9 U. S. Steel pfd.	12,700.	12,650.
10 Republic Steel com.	4,812.50	4,737.50
	214,025.	212,162.50

Divided by 20 gives average price   107.01   106.08

To find the mean price, add the average highest and lowest together and divide by 2, viz.:

Average Highest   107.0125
Average Lowest   106.0812

213.09

Divide by 2 and you have
the mean price   106.54

Then construct a chart on paper regularly ruled for the purpose.* Divide by vertical figures into days, make dots at the high, low and mean points each day and draw lines to connect the respective dots. Lines showing the highest and lowest should be light and the trend line heavy.

The mean price is our Trend Indicator and its movements should be closely watched and interpreted along the lines suggested at the beginning of this article.

*Check-ruled drawing paper can be obtained at any stationer's.

This Trend Indicator should show accurately whether the market is to go up or down from any given point.

It should forecast the main movement for from a few days to a week ahead, barring accidents.

It will not predict catastrophes such as the San Francisco fire, the sudden death of a magnate, the assassination of a great ruler, or an unexpected threat of war. All these come under the head of accidents.

Now see the advantage of this Trend Indicator. Each person can figure it out

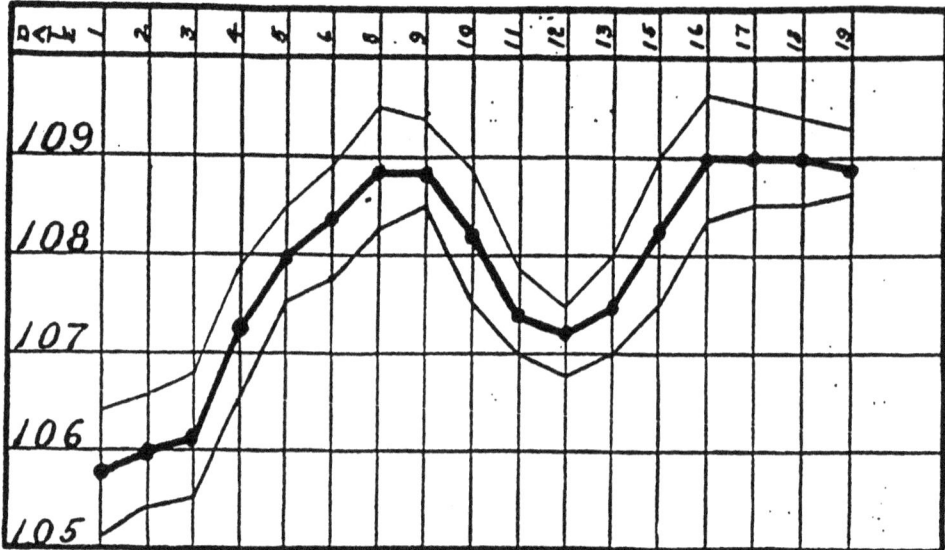

MECHANICAL TREND INDICATO R.

for himself and make his own deductions. The more expert he becomes in following its guidance, the greater his profits.

All commitments are made with strict regard to this trend. If the trend is upward, the operator watches for weak spots on which to buy. He never sells short against the trend. If the chart indicates a down trend, he plays the short side, watching for temporarily strong periods when his sales may be made to best advantage. When he is in doubt he either waits or closes out everything until the trend becomes clear.

Having one's own Trend Indicator eliminates the tip, for the Indicator will tell more truthfully what the market will do than any so-called good judges of the market. It also enables one to discard newspaper opinion and gossip, as well as other misleading factors too numerous to mention.

[CONTINUED IN THE JANUARY ISSUE.]

N. B.—Readers are advised to keep complete files of The Wall Street Journal, or any other newspaper reporting each transaction, so that examples given may be studied and acted upon.

How to Select Investments

By WILLIAM WALKER

II.—Characteristics of a Good Investment

HAVING divided your capital into two parts, approximately equal—a reserve or investment fund and a speculative fund—you are then ready to select the securities in which your investments shall be made.

It is important to have a clear understanding of the general characteristics of a good investment and the rights of the investor. There are only three kinds of securities:

1. Some sort of promise to pay—a bond, mortgage, note, or loan on collateral.

2. An equity, by which the purchaser becomes the owner of a fractional part of the company—a certain number of *shares*.

3. A security which is convertible from one of the above forms into the other under certain conditions specified on the face of the security itself.

VARYING CHARACTER OF SECURITIES

Now it might seem at first glance as though this general division of securities would correspond almost exactly to the division of our capital into an investment and a speculative fund. The bonds, notes, or other promises to pay might seem to be investments, and the equities or *shares* would seem to be speculative, as their value depends upon the success of the business.

This will not do, howver, for some stocks are far safer than some bonds; and at certain times and under certain conditions *any* standard dividend-paying stock is better than *any* standard bond.

For example, the stock of the Pennsylvania Railroad, which has paid dividends steadily for about fifty years, is a much safer investment than the bonds of a new road which is barely meeting fixed charges and might be thrown into

the hands of a receiver by a few years of hard times. It is customary to recommend bonds as a woman's investment and for trust funds, etc., but there are bonds and bonds; and there are some stocks which represent enterprises so firmly established that the shares sell on an income basis as low as that of high grade bonds.

Likewise, in a period of rising prices for commodities, like the present, all lines of business become very prosperous. Profits, as measured in dollars, are large, and all stocks, being equities, or fractional parts of an enterprise, have improved dividend prospects and consequently rise in price. On the other hand, the very activity of business increases the demand for money and this raises the rate for money in the general money market, so that a bond, bearing a fixed rate of interest, does not give as good returns as money otherwise invested. The holders of the bonds sell out and invest their money elsewhere, and the bond, as a result, declines in value.

At such a time any sound investment stock is better to hold than any bond—and this wholly without reference to the amount of security behind the bond. It is not a question of security, it is a question of the rate for money.

It is evident, therefore, that discrimination must be exercised in the placing of both your investment fund and your speculative fund. No simple rule will cover the case.

CLASSIFICATION OF SECURITIES.

A *mortgage bond* is merely a mortgage split up into convenient units so that it can be more readily sold and transferred. Each bond is a certain fraction of the entire mortgage, just as each share of stock is a fraction in the ownership of the company. The mortgage bond is based upon definite, specified security. This may be a "general lien," covering all the property of the company, and usually subject to some "prior liens"; or the mortgage may cover only a certain part of the company's holdings, specified therein.

A *debenture bond*, on the other hand, is scarcely a bond at all—it is practically a note, collectable from the company just as any note is collectable from an individual.

The interest of an *income bond* is payble out of the company's income. If the company has no income it defaults the interest, but this does not throw the company into the hands of a receiver. In other words the income bond is in much the same position as the stock, except that the dividend on the income bond will not be increased beyond the rate specified in the bond, while there is no such limit to possible dividends on the stock.

An *equipment bond* is a lien on certain specified equipment, and is usually paid off in instalments as the equipment depreciates through service.

The *collateral trust bond,* as its name indicates, is secured by specified collateral placed in trust for the benefit of the bondholders.

A *convertible bond* may be converted into stock under certain conditions which are specified on its face—usually at a fixed price and under certain limitations as to date.

There is practically no limit to the number of different kinds of bonds which may be issued, depending on the nature of the security and the character of the lien upon such security.

Varieties of stock are few in number, as all stock must represent a share in the business. Preferred stock is entitled to full dividends before the common receives any dividends, and if the preferred is cumulative all dividends in arrears on the preferred must be paid before any distribution can be made on the common. If the preferred is noncumulative, whatever dividends are passed will not be made up in the future, but all additional earnings over the amount to which the preferred is entitled year by year will go to the common.

Before going further a brief discussion of the general characteristics of a good investment is necessary.

I. SAFETY

It is often assumed that funds may be so invested as to assure absolute safety. In fact, there is nothing "absolute" outside of the science of mathematics—everything is comparative. The element of risk is always present, though it may be in very small degree.

"Safety" means different things for different people. For a widow, left with a small property on which to support and educate her children, safety means an investment which can be left to itself year after year and can be depended upon to yield a certain, definite income. For a business man who is investing his surplus, who is not dependent upon his interest money for his living, who can exercise some judgment as to the business situation and who has the advantage of sound advice on market conditions, the word safety covers a much broader range. He is warranted in taking a "business man's risk."

There is one important element in safety, which is little understood by most investors, and yet has a most far-reaching influence—the purchasing power of money.

One might suppose, for example, that nothing could be safer than consols—the consolidated bonds of the British Empire. Yet in recent years they have proved far from safe, if safety is to mean the maintenance of capital as well as an assured interest. Consols have suffered a severe decline since the period of the Boer War. While England's increasing indebtedness doubtless has its influence on the price of consols, it is generally believed that the great increase in the production of gold is the most important factor. This has brought about rising prices and active business, thus tempting a large number of investors to sell their "promises to pay" a certain amount of gold at a specified date, and to invest their money in "equities," where they will get the advantage of the great increase in the value of the property as measured in gold. As consols yielded a very low rate of interest, they were among the first to be disposed of, and such sales have naturally had a depressing effect on the price.

The safety of an investment, therefore, cannot be judged solely by the amount of security back of it. Safety against a decline in price is equally important.

There is also a distinction to be drawn between safety of principal and safety of interest. Suppose a great railway guarantees the interest on the stock of a branch line for a period of twenty years. The interest is safe, but what will be the value of the principal at the end of the twenty years?

On the other hand, suppose the bond of a real estate company is secured by twice its value of unimproved real estate, yet at the moment the company has no earnings owing to business depression. The interest on the bond may be defaulted and the company forced into the hands of a receiver; yet the principal is safe enough if the investor can afford to hold on.

2. RATE OF INTEREST

All the world knows that, as a rule, the lower the interest yield on the price of a security the safer the investment. This is only saying that investors will be content with a smaller return from an investment which they consider to have the highest degree of safety.

Yet the judgment of the crowd is far from being always right. United States Steel preferred sold at 50 in 1903, although paying 7 per cent. dividends on par and 14 per cent. on the price. Subsequent events have proved that these dividends were not only assured, but that the security behind them was being enormously increased year by year. Seaboard Air Line 1st 4s sold at 92 in 1905; yet the road went into the hands of a receiver and these bonds went down to 43 in 1908—a decline of over 50 per cent. The buyers of these bonds at 92 were very seriously in error.

You may reply that on the *known facts* at the time, the Seaboard bonds were worth 92 in 1905 and the Steel preferred was worth only 50 in 1903; but you would have hard work to prove your case.

Investors, like everybody else, labor under what may be called "the delusion of fixed ideas." That is, they fail to examine each individual security on its merits, but roughly apply certain preconceived notions to all securities alike. They know that the security labeled "bond" precedes the security labeled "stock" as a lien on the property; hence the word "bond" adds something to the value. They know that railroad securities as a rule are safer than industrial securities as a rule; hence the word "railroad" adds something to the value. They are intensely conservative and prefer old and long established companies; hence the securities of a new company are at a disadvantage, no matter how excellent they may be. And it is precisely this lack of originality and failure to investigate and discriminate on the part of the vast majority, that enables the investor of active mind and sound judgment to realize a larger return on his capital.

3. SALABILITY

Many persons find it necessary to hold only securities which are readily salable on short notice. They must be salable not only in good times but in panics, as the panic is likely to be just the time when the owner might find himself over-extended or involved in outside operations, and might therefore require the use of the funds represented by his securities.

This fact adds to the price of securities having a broad and ready market, beyond the price at which they would naturally sell as a result of safety of capital and rate of interest. For this reason the investor who can be certain of his ability to hold securities until a favorable market can be obtained, may often pick out a better bargain by selecting a security which is little known and has a narrow market.

For the reserve fund previously referred to, salability is of little importance provided the value is there. Inactivity is no bar in considering purchases to go into this fund. It may be an advantage and it may not. Some securities are inactive because they are scarce and closely held. They may even be higher in proportion to their value than other securities having a broader market. But there is another class of stocks and bonds which are inactive because little known, or because no special effort has been made to bring them to the attention of investors. Such securities are likely to return a relatively higher rate of interest in proportion to their value and soundness.

Many irrigation and waterpower stocks and bonds belong to this class. Small companies whose field of operation is distant from the principal stock markets are likely to be in this class, because they are less easily investigated than larger corporations or those nearer at hand.

A few years ago Sears, Roebuck & Company preferred stock was a good example of a little-known security returning a large interest rate and amply secured. The company was doing an enormous business, was rapidly extending its field of operations, and had a "good will" asset the value of which it would be impossible to estimate. Yet little was heard of the stock and it was selling relatively low. More recently Mr. Sears has sold his interest in the company to New York capitalists and the stock has been brought into public notice with a corresponding advance in prices.

For your speculative fund inactive securities will not do. The first essential for that fund is a ready market. The first of a series of "golden rules," used by a well known capitalist in his market operations, is said to be: "Never speculate in an inactive security." And even though the primary purpose of your speculative fund is to yield a good rate of interest, you cannot afford to include in it anything that cannot be sold promptly if desired.

4. SPECULATIVE POSSIBILITIES

On neither your reserve fund nor your speculative fund can you afford to neglect speculative possibilities. No matter what security you buy, you are certain of one thing—if there is any public market for it; it is going to fluctuate. All its fluctuations mean profit or loss to you; therefore you must consider them. This applies to government bonds and Steel common, though not in the same degree.

Your consideration of speculative possibilities will, however, be entirely different for the two funds. For your reserve fund you are seeking chiefly to avoid loss. You will endeavor to select securities of the strongest possible character which you believe to be certain to maintain a range of prices as high as you have paid. Safety is your principal consideration for this fund. But for your speculative fund you will try to purchase securities which will not only yield a good interest return but will also advance in price within a period of a few years.

When we talk about speculation in connection with investments we do not mean "taking chances." On the contrary the whole effort of the investor will be to speculate so shrewdly as to avoid taking chances. The first and original meaning of the word speculate is "to pursue inquiries and form conjectures on any object in one's mind." The word is derived from the Latin *specculor*, to behold. As applied to investments, "speculate" is nearly equivalent to "foresee."

In this sense almost every act of life is or should be based upon speculation; and most of all the investment of hard-earned savings, or capital upon which your future and that of your family is dependent.

It has been said that the rich can afford to take chances but do not, while the poor cannot afford to take chances, but do. One of the main purposes of this series of articles is to aid persons of moderate income in avoiding the taking of dangerous chances.

The next article of this series will contain practical hints on the choice of securities for a reserve fund.

The Bargain Indicator

Some Notable Changes

NOTE.—Except where otherwise noted, earnings are herein computed for the twelve latest months available, thus keeping the table constantly up-to-date. Additions and betterments are included in the earnings as given, wherever they are so reported as to be distinguishable from ordinary expenses of maintenance, since earnings invested in the improvement of the property are usually of more value to the stockholders in the long run than if they had been distributed as dividends. Such additions and betterments out of current earnings increase the equity of the stockholders and therefore render the stock more valuable.

As this magazine is mailed to subscribers two or three days before it appears on the news stands, subscribers get the first advantage of the Bargain Indicator.

Railroads

Buffalo, Rochester & Pittsburg common advances to third place this month, owing to continued heavy earnings. The merits of a relatively small road like this are often temporarily overlooked by investors. The preferred has paid 6 per cent. regularly since 1900. The common paid 6 per cent. in 1904, 1905 and 1906, 5½ per cent. in 1907, 4½ in 1908, and 4 in 1909. Earnings are now picking up again.

Toledo, St. Louis & Western made an even better showing in its annual report, received since our last issue, than had been calculated from current earnings. Of course its dividends from its holdings of Alton are the most important feature.

Louisville & Nashville is earning as much as ever on par, and drops to fifth place only because it has been crowded down by the advances of others. The same is true of the four roads which follow it in the table.

Chicago & Alton's sudden drop is the most surprising feature of the month. The annual report, just published, shows unexpected increases in various items of expense. The most remarkable is an increase of $200,000 in "Hire of Equipment and Rentals." The result is that although "Total Net Income" is about as anticipated, the unexpected deductions reduce the amount applicable to dividends. However, Alton's expenditures for new construction, additions and improvements, during the year were $968,000, much of which was spent on grade reduction and double tracking and will eventually reduce operating expenses. Current earnings are falling off a trifle as compared with last year.

Pennsylvania rises a few points, chiefly because of the fall in the price of the stock owing to the issue of rights.

Kansas City Southern is showing a decline in net earnings in recent months. This road has been acquired by the Hill interests, and it is probable that a greater proportion of gross earnings is being applied to maintenance of way and structures than was formerly the case.

Chicago, Milwaukee & St. Paul owes its low position to the financing of the Puget Sound Extension, earnings from which have not yet been made public.

Industrials

U. S. Steel common is the feature of the industrial list, jumping to fourth place as a result of heavy earnings during the last quarter.

American Malt preferred, for which the annual report is now at hand, takes a good position.

Pacific Coast common advances, owing to large recent earnings.

International Harvester common drops six places, because of an advance in the price of the stock.

THE BARGAI

TABLE SHOWING WHICH STOCK

RAILROADS

PRESENT EARNING POWER AS COMPARED WITH MARKET PRICE

Position.		Approximate earnings on par.	Price Nov. 11, '09.	Earnings on price.
1	Detroit United	10.6%	62	17.1%
2	Rock Island common	4.9	40	12.2
3	Buffalo, Rochester & Pittsburg common	10.9	98	11.1
4	Toledo, St. Louis & Western common	(d) 5.7	54	10.5
5	Louisville & Nashville	15.6	151	10.3
6	Union Pacific com.	20.0	200	10.0
7	Norfolk & Western com.	9.5	95	10.0
8	Colorado & Southern com.	5.3	56	9.5
9	Atchison com.	(a)10.7	119	9.0
10	Chesapeake & Ohio	7.5	87	8.6
11	Delaware, Lackawanna & Western	45.9	566	8.1
12	Reading com.	(c)13.0	161	8.1
13	Pennsylvania	11.4	140	8.1
14	Southern Pacific com.	10.5	129	8.1
15	Pittsburg, Cin., Chicago & St. Louis com.	(b) 7.7	95	8.1
16	Atlantic Coast Line Railroad	10.8	136	7.9
17	Minneapolis, St. Paul & S. S. M. com.	10.7	135	7.9
18	St. Louis Southwestern pfd.	4.8	68	7.1
19	Kansas City Southern com.	3.0	44	6.8
20	Twin City Rapid Transit	7.3	109	6.7
21	Delaware & Hudson	12.1	184	6.6
22	Chicago & Northwestern com.	12.1	187	6.5
23	Great Northern pfd.	9.1	142	6.4
24	Northern Pacific com.	(a) 9.1	145	6.3
25	Baltimore & Ohio com.	7.3	116	6.3
26	New York, New Haven & Hartford	9.1	155	5.9
27	New York Central	7.7	132	5.8
28	Chicago & Alton com.	3.9	68	5.8
29	Brooklyn Rapid Transit	4.1	75	5.5
30	Canadian Pacific	9.8	184	5.3
31	Illinois Central	7.5	146	5.1
32	Missouri Pacific	3.4	70	4.9
33	New York, Ontario & Western	2.1	46	4.6
34	Wabash pfd.	2.2	51	4.3
35	Cleveland, Cincinnati, Chicago & St. Louis com.	3.1	78	4.0
36	Missouri, Kansas & Texas com.	(e) 1.9	47	4.0
37	Denver & Rio Grande com.	1.7	46	3.7
38	Minneapolis & St. Louis com.	1.9	53	3.6
39	Southern Railway com.	0.8	30	2.7
40	Chicago, Minneapolis & St. Paul com.	(a) 3.9	156	2.5
41	Erie common	0.6	32	1.9
42	Wisconsin Central com.	.0	51	.0
43	Iowa Central pfd.	.0	51	.0
44	Texas & Pacific	.0	35	.0
45	St. Louis Southwestern com.	.0	30	.0
46	Duluth, South Shore & Atlantic pfd.	.0	29	.0
47	Wabash common	.0	20	.0

(a) On increased capitalization. (b) Pfd. and com. share equally after com. receives 5%.
(c) Includes betterments on subsidiary companies. (d) Includes income from Alton divs.
(e) Betterments north of Red River not included.

INDICATOR

ARE THE BEST PURCHASES NOW

INDUSTRIALS, &c.

BASED ON LATEST OFFICIAL REPORTS

Pos.	Date of Report.			Approximate earnings on par.	Price Nov. 11, '09.	Earnings on price.
1	June	30,	1909	Colorado Fuel & Iron pfd.	(d)42.9%	110	39.0%
2	June	30,	1909	Amer. Hide & Leather pfd.	(a)10.8	47	23.0
3	June	30,	1909	Amer. Agricultural Chem. com.	7.5	48	15.6
4	Sept.	30,	1909	U. S. Steel com.	(b)13.5	89	15.2
5	Mar.	31,	1909	Amer. Beet Sugar com.	7.0	47	14.9
6	May	31,	1909	Virginia-Carolina Chem. com.	7.1	49	14.5
7	July	31,	1909	Amer. Linseed pfd.	5.8	42	13.8
8	Aug.	31,	1908	Amer. Malt Corp. pfd.	6.2	48	12.9
9	Apr.	30,	1909	U. S. Realty & Improvement	(c) 9.7	82	11.8
10	Feb.	28,	1909	Corn Products pfd.	(a) 9.5	86	11.0
11	Jan.	31,	1909	Union Bag & Paper pfd.	(a) 7.1	75	9.5
12	Aug.	31,	1909	Pacific Coast com.	(c) 9.8	107	9.2
13	Aug.	31,	1909	Sloss-Sheffield com.	(b) 8.2	90	9.1
14	Mar.	31,	1909	U. S. Rubber com.	4.0	49	8.2
15	Sept.	30,	1909	Western Union.	(b) 6.2	77	8.1
16	Apr.	30,	1909	Amer. Smelt. & Ref. com.	7.7	98	7.8
17	Dec.	31,	1908	Amer. Can pfd.	6.6	85	7.3
18	June	30,	1909	Republic Iron & Steel pfd.	8.0	105	7.6
19	Dec.	31,	1908	Inter. Harvester com.	7.8	107	7.3
20	Dec.	31,	1908	People's Gas	7.8	114	6.9
21	Dec.	31,	1908	National Lead com.	5.8	87	6.7
22	Jan.	31,	1909	National Biscuit com.	7.4	114	6.5
23	Sept.	30,	1909	Amer. Tel. & Tel.	(c) 8.7	141	6.2
24	June	30,	1909	Distillers' Securities	2.3	37	6.2
25	Dec.	31,	1908	North American	4.8	79	6.1
26	Dec.	31,	1908	Amer. Sugar Ref. com.	7.5	131	5.7
27	Dec.	31,	1908	Railway Steel Spring pfd.	5.6	108	5.2
28	June	30,	1909	National En. & Stamping com.	1.1	21	5.2
29	Jan.	31,	1909	General Electric	7.4	162	4.6
30	Dec.	31,	1908	Utah Copper (Par $10)	23.3	$52	4.5
31	Dec.	31,	1908	Tennessee Copper (Par $25)	6.5	$36	4.5
32	June	30,	1909	International Paper pfd.	2.7	61	4.4
33	Feb.	1,	1909	Mackay com.	4.0	93	4.3
34	Dec.	31,	1908	Bethlehem Steel pfd.	2.4	66	3.6
35	June	30,	1909	Amer. Locomotive pfd.	4.00	115	3.5
36	Apr.	30,	1909	Amer. Car & Foundry com.	2.6	74	3.5
37	Dec.	31,	1908	Amer. Woolen pfd.	3.2	103	3.1
38	Dec.	31,	1908	Consolidated Gas	4.1	144	2.8
39	Dec.	31,	1908	Central Leather com.	1.3	47	2.8
40	Apr.	30,	1909	Amalgamated Copper	2.4	89	2.7
41	Mar.	31,	1909	Inter. Steam Pump com.	1.4	54	2.6
42	Dec.	31,	1908	New York Air Brake	2.4	95	2.5
43	May	31,	1909	U. S. Cast Iron Pipe pfd.	1.3	87	1.5
44	June	30,	1909	Allis-Chalmers pfd.	0.8	54	1.5
45	Dec.	31,	1908	Pressed Steel Car pfd.	1.2	105	1.1
46	July	31,	1909	Amer. Steel Foundries	0.7	65	1.1
47	June	30,	1909	Amer. Locomotive com.	.0	62	.0
48	Dec.	31,	1908	Pressed Steel Car com.	.0	52	.0
49	Dec.	31,	1908	Railway Steel Spring com.	.0	49	.0
50	June	30,	1909	Republic Iron & Steel com.	.0	47	.0
51	Dec.	31,	1908	Amer. Woolen com.	.0	35	.0
52	Dec.	31,	1908	Bethlehem Steel com.	.0	35	.0
53	May	31,	1909	U. S. Cast Iron Pipe com.	.0	33	.0
54	Feb.	28,	1909	Corn Products com.	.0	22	.0
55	July	31,	1909	Amer. Linseed com.	.0	16	.0
56	June	30,	1909	International Paper com.	.0	15	.0
57	Dec.	31,	1908	Amer. Can com.	.0	14	.0
58	Jan.	31,	1909	Union Bag & Paper com.	.0	14	.0

(a) Divs. in arrears. (b) Based on quarterly report. (c) Based on current reports. (d) Divs. in arrears; stock very inactive.

A Sign of Bull Moves

Explanation of a Principle Which Shows When Stocks Are Scarce

By FRANK H. TUBBS

AFTER the great depression of 1907 it was evident that a large number of investors had learned the lesson which gave them the right time for buying stocks. The lists of stockholders of all substantial corporations were greatly enlarged.

There was a principle underlying the buying. A principle demonstrates in an idea. Conversely the successful application of an idea demonstrates the existence of the principle. It is worth while to investigate the principle, with its idea, which underlay the successful purchases of stock in the winter of 1907-8 to see if the same cannot be utilized in 1909-10.

It requires great patience to wait for another panic which will carry prices down so that stocks are on the bargain counter, and many can't wait. If there is anything in the principle which once proved right, and if it can be applied often, speculators want to know it. We believe there is something in it and that it can be used several times on every long swing of the market, and we will endeavor to make it plain.

A principle is a fixed thing. It is right. Further, it applies to small matters as to great. There is underlying principle in mathematics. That science is the most exact of all thus far discovered by man. He who has educated himself best in that science knows best how to apply it. The farther he has risen in his researches the broader the possibility of application. One who understands dissection of the sphere knows more of the underlying principle of mathematics than does he who knows only plain surfaces. He who knows only the skeleton of mathematics—addition, subtraction, multiplication and division—cannot use the *principle* of mathematics. Yet the principle is there and it is open to mastery. Ignorance only keeps all from applying the principle.

Ignorance has been defined as ignoring facts pertinent to the subject.

This preliminary is given to impress the truth that that which permitted thousands to make money in stocks after the panic of 1907, understood and applied as a principle, would permit the continuance of money-making. Also, that the more thoroughly the principle is studied the better it can be used.

Further, that those who do not use it permit themselves to remain in ignorance (ignoring the facts as to this principle). The very fact that they will not go in for serious study is in itself a proof of ignorance.

There can be no large advance in the stock market, nor in individual stocks, so long as large quantities of stock are pressing for sale.

The decline of 1907 was begun by throwing over stocks. It had interruptions caused by cessation of selling. Whenever selling was resumed from any source, a "slump" followed. Scarcity of available funds prevented purchases of stock. The decline was bound to continue until the stage was reached where those who still had money took whatever stock was offered. In the case of the decline of 1907, it was the small investor who really stopped the decline. He came in and took fractional lots, even down to one share, until stocks became hard to get. Further liquidation was not forthcoming. Buyers enough were present to take all offerings. This stopped the decline.

Therein is the principle. We will show how it has worked since 1907, how it may be expected to work in the future and the way to utilize it.

Many people date the bottom of the panic October 24, 1907, the day when Mr. Morgan spectacularly threw several millions of dollars into the loan crowd to stay liquidation. But that was not the end, because the "principle" had not worked out. The mere fact that it was necessary to stop by extraordinary means the downward rush, shows that date was not the end. Mr. Morgan's action merely served to prevent dumping by large speculators who lacked money to carry their stocks.

The lesser liquidation was not complete until November 21, 1907. Even that date may be too early, for the full working of the "principle" was not met until March 2, 1908. As that was the time when there appeared a perfect demonstration of the fact that buying had completely overcome liquidation, and that the market had returned to conditions of normal speculation, we will use the period around March, 1908, as an illustration.

The evidence of the mastery of buying over selling was contained in lessening daily volumes for a period of about three weeks—February 10 to March 2.

To find such evidence one must keep a record which shows a plain picture of an average of the market. The average given by the "Twenty Railroads" as published in the *Wall Street Journal*, gives the evidence. This is mentioned as the readiest way of showing how to keep an "averaging" chart. For myself, I do not use the "Twenty Railroad" average, for I think a simpler way does just as well. The most perfect "averaging" chart is one composed of all the usually active stocks, railroad and industrial, using forty or fifty stocks in the list. That would comprise about one-third of the list daily traded in. But that is cumbersome and is irksome to keep.

I find that a combination of the active railroad stocks gives a very good line on the market and it is from the chart based on this combination that I will illustrate.

During the latter part of January and early February, 1908, the average fluctuation of each day had been running from 2.34 to 3.67 points a day. The "average," it may be explained for clearness, is obtained by adding the highs for the day of the stocks composing the combination, which gives the "average" high of the day; then, adding the lows of the day of the same stocks, gives the "average" lows of the day. The difference between the two gives the "average" fluctuation of the day.

Now, in the period before February 10, 1908, the average fluctuation per day had been 2.34 to 3.67 points. From February 10 it began to lessen. On that day, February 10, it was 2.34. Daily fluctuations gradually lessened, reaching the lowest February 28, a Friday, when it was down to .60 point, less than ⅝ of a point. Could there be better evidence that the supply of stocks was exhausted? The average daily fluctuation over the period from February 10 to March 2, was 1.41 of a point. In the last eight days of this period they ran 1.02, .80, 1.15, .81, .73, .60, 1.05, 1, all below the average of the period.

This is given as an illustration. Whenever similar cases occur, the speculator may feel well assured that the "principle" is at work. It only requires some little buying from any source at such a time to put the market up.

One may rest assured that manipulators always know such a condition and that they will utilize it. First, they will "run in the shorts." No matter what any one says there is always a short interest in the market and after every depression there is always an interest which believes the market is going lower and they will stay short until forced to cover. Manipulators build on stubborn human nature. After the shorts are run in, the manipulators buy to make a further rise.

The question will arise "Will the principle work often and at every level of prices?" It works on any level. It may seem as if "stocks are very high." Recently we have had a higher level for the most active stocks than was ever before known in the history of Wall Street. It seems to old speculators, at such time, that stocks cannot go higher. But if there is scarcity of stocks, as demonstrated by lessening average fluctuations over a period long enough to furnish suitable demonstrations, prices will go higher, barring "earthquake, calamity or sudden death."

There is no limit to the top, as is illustrated when a stock is cornered and there is demand for it. With enormous possibilities in American wealth, which is eventually turned into speculation, one cannot measure the possibilities of rise. Many stocks, although they have been, or are, high, yet double and treble in price. That is possible, and when they demonstrate, by narrowness of average daily fluctuation, that they cannot be had in quantity, they will go higher from any level.

We will now see if the principle works often. In the last of March, 1908, daily fluctuations had elongated till they reached 2.51 points. From there they gradually lessened until April 22, when they reached the remarkably small range of .39, or about three-eighths point for a whole day's trading. Then the market rose.

On May 20, 1908, fluctuations had again elongated to 3.75 points and on several days they were about 3 points. From then they lessened until on July 1, 2 and 3, they were .42, .29 and .24. Only one-fourth point a day. Certainly no stock was coming out. The market rose after the "Fourth of July" holiday.

Again, in the latter part of October, up to the days just before the national election, daily fluctuations narrowed down, and for about ten days they averaged one point or less per day. We all recall what happened right after Mr. Taft was elected.

On February 23, 1909, fluctuations had elongated till they reached 4.01 points, only to narrow again to March 15, when they were down to .84. On May 3, 1909, they were up to 2.08, and on May 28, down to .56. Another rise. On June 21, they were up to 2.70; on July 10, down to .62. On July 21, risen to 1.30; on July 26, down to .76.

Here, then, we have had eight times in a little over seventeen months when we have had the evidence which demonstrates our principle given plainly and every time it has been followed by a rising market.

The question may come into the minds of some readers whether this plan will work in bear markets. It is very doubtful if such a series of narrowing days as would lead investors to think it a buying time could occur in a bear market.

The only series which approaches having the appearance of a buying time within the period of my observation, from which there was a decline, was along in June, 1907. There were seven

days of narrow market, which might have given reason for buying. They were followed by a rise extending to July 26, amounting to eight points, in the average. That was enough for profit and if it were not taken, surely the investor would not have permitted a loss when his stock returned to the buying point.

When speaking of average drops, we must remember that in striking an average we are using stocks which are very speculative. They are not the ones which investors would be likely to use. Such stocks as they would select for purchases, probably the dividend-yielding, seasoned stocks, would have less decline than even the "average" drop of a group of speculative stocks. If the drop in the latter class was five points, that of more strictly investment stocks would be but two or three.

No one expects to buy right at the bottom. Even in buying in the great panic of 1907, investors were prepared to see their stocks go lower and often they did go lower. Many went five or ten points below where purchases were made.

What I contend is that a prolonged series of narrowing days, coming down so that the average range per day of a group of active stocks becomes less than one point, demonstrates that stocks are scarce and that scarcity will necessarily produce a rise. Purchases during the scarcity will yield profits. That there may be a dip is possible, but for this the investor is prepared.

Naturally, when our principle shows its work after a protracted decline, there is the greatest probability of large profits. But more moderate profits can come every time the principle has a chance to demonstrate itself. It is also probable that, in trading on this idea, when the market has had two years of constant ascent with little reaction, it is well to place a limit to the risk assumed by placing stop-loss a few points under where purchase is made. That was not necessary in November, 1907.

It is also evident that profits in rises after two years of bullishness are to be taken oftener than they were soon after the panic. We have had four rises in seven months of 1907, and in the whole year of 1908 we had but three.

The Ethics of Speculation

By THOMAS F. WOODLOCK*

In considering the ethics of speculation it is quite clear that under no conditions can such things as "wash sales" or "manipulations" with intent to deceive be defended, or regarded as anything but immoral in the full sense of the word. The ethical questions that we have to consider are all based on the assumption of a free open market—a market in other words, where contracts are made without the use of force or fraud.

Speculation can be ethically considered under two aspects, viz:, first, in relation to the body politic, second, in relation to the individual speculator. And in considering it economically we must remember that while good morals may not always be economically valuable, bad morals cannot be good economics.

There is much popular confusion of mind as to both speculation and gambling, many people considering the terms synonymous and the thing implied by both morally wrong. We have already seen the nature of the distinction between the two ideas. But as a matter of fact neither is morally wrong in itself; there is nothing necessarily evil in a gambling contract, for the law which forbids certain kinds of gambling permits others, which it could not do if gambling were a *malum in se*. Clearly, therefore, there is nothing wrong in speculation as such.

The law aims to prohibit certain forms of gambling which serve no economic purpose on the ground that experience demonstrates damage to the individual without compensating economic value. The first important thing to note as to speculation is that it performs certain valuable economic functions, viz:

a. It is the main factor in maintaining a free and wide market for securities.

b. It is the main factor in the process of adjustment of security prices to values, and

c. It is the largest individual factor in promoting the development of corporate enterprise.

Without speculation, a free market and a wide market would be impossible. Experience shows that the less speculation there is in a stock, the more restricted is the market and the more violent the fluctuations in price. For while speculation tends to increase the number of fluctuations in price, it tends also to diminish their intensity.

Speculation continually tends to adjust prices to values, and this is an economic process of some importance to the community, for by this means the market is kept not only free and wide but also true. Of course, the excesses of speculation obscure this process at times and temporarily impair its value, but by no means destroy it.

Speculation tends to promote corporate enterprise by keeping capital constantly pioneering, so to speak, and constantly pushing the outposts of civilization further into the jungle. The railroads of this country never would have reached their present development without speculation.

Remembering that the market for securities is an absolute necessity for the success of a system of corporate enterprise and that the market practically depends upon speculation for its very existence, it is impossible to think of corporate enterprise without unhindered and untrammeled speculation.

It must further be noted that in this country the keystone of our banking system is the New York call-money market, and this call-money market absolutely depends on the Stock Exchange for its existence.

Now, remembering the nature of the distinction between speculation and gambling as previously made, it is evident that mere stock gambling, as distinct from stock speculation, fails to fulfil two

*From a series of lectures delivered at the New York Y. M. C. A.

of the three functions above enumerated as economically valuable. It *does* help to make the market free and wide, but it clearly does not help to adjust prices to values save accidentally; nor does it help much in the pioneering of capital. On the other hand, by its excesses and its mistakes it actually hinders or tends to hinder in both the latter cases. It may be admitted without qualification that the nearer stock speculation approaches to stock gambling, the less economically valuable it is.

Some people say, admitting the economic value of stock speculation, would it not be well to find some way of stopping stock gambling while permitting stock speculation of a legitimate kind. Unfortunately this is impossible.

The reason it is impossible is in the rather important fact that the distinction between speculation and gambling in stocks is not in the nature of the act performed, but in the person performing it. What is gambling on A's part may be perfectly legitimate speculation on the part of B, and no good can be found in law to prevent A from doing what B is permitted to do, for neither A's nor B's mind can be put in evidence.

There is no way in law to stop stock gambling without at the same time stopping stock speculation, and stopping stock speculation means practical destruction of the market for securities, or at least the driving it elsewhere. Both stand or fall together. Those who desire to abolish stock speculation because of the danger to the individual should logically propose abolition of railroads or diminution of the speed of trains because people are killed on railroads—or abolition of newspapers for fear of scandalizing people. The law cannot, and I believe should not attempt to save people from the simple consequence of their own cupidity and ignorance. All that it can reasonably do is protect business contracts as far as possible from fraud or duress.

Concluding, therefore, that stock speculation, even with its concomitant gambling abuses, is legitimately and economically to exist, we have to consider the ethics of the question from the standpoint of the individual himself. We may most conveniently do so in the form of questions, viz.:

a. Is one morally entitled to gamble in stocks?

b. What qualifications entitle one morally to speculate in stocks?

c. What considerations limit one thus qualified in his speculations?

It is not difficult to answer the first question and the answer must be that while theoretically one may gamble in stocks as in any other way, practically stock-gambling falls under the general rule as to the kind of gambling prohibited by law as bad for the individual and not economically valuable to the community.

We can imagine a case where a man might without moral transgression gamble in stocks in that he fulfilled all the requirements laid down by moralists for legitimate gambling; but experience would show such cases to be very few and far between. As a matter of fact, stock gambling almost invariably involves risking sums utterly disproportionate to the means of the gamblers, thus breaking a fundamental law of justice. It is safe to go on the principle that no one is morally entitled to gamble in stocks.

To speculate legitimately, a man must possess:

a. Knowledge of what he is doing so that he acts reasonably.

b. Sufficient capital to give him with this knowledge such reasonable prospect of success as warrants him in considering speculation as a business enterprise.

A man who speculates legitimately must be able to reckon his chances intelligently so that his deductions can be defended at the bar of common sense. It is this intelligent attempt at foresight which makes legitimate speculation out of what would otherwise be mere gaming.

Secondly, he must make his commitments in a business-like way, suiting them to his capital—cutting his coat according to his cloth—and to the anticipated risks. Otherwise he would not be acting in a business-like way and would in a very real sense be gambling. Many men all versed in the principles of price movement are driven by cupidity into what are practically gambling transactions in this way: they possess one of the two qualifications but not the other.

Now comes the question of ethical considerations which limit a man thus qualified in his speculations. The most important of these is the matter of trust relations, i. e., relations existing between him and others which prevent him from profiting at their expense. The principal instance of this is the relation of directors to stockholders.

All are agreed that no man has a right to take advantage of his partner by reason of knowledge acquired by him as a partner to buy from or sell to him his interest in the partnership while keeping him in ignorance of this knowledge—even if no actual positive misrepresentation of facts is made.

But it is sometimes argued the existence of a free and open market for securities destroys altogether the trust-relationship between individuals who are stockholders and directors in a concern and abolishes the duties of one to another growing out of such relationship.

The existence of the open market, with buyers and sellers always present, undoubtedly to some extent weakens, at least in practice, their relations, inasmuch as it obviates the necessity of private personal negotiations which would otherwise be necessary. Moreover buyers and sellers in an open market by implication may possibly be held to waive some of their rights in this respect by their open bids and offers.

Yet that these relations are not wholly destroyed is evinced by the fact that public opinion would not tolerate the action of directors who would speculate upon the strength of a dividend just ordered by them, but not yet announced to the public.

The fact is that public opinion while reprobating the most flagrant breaks of trust of this sort permits a good deal of latitude in the matter, and considers as not *dishonest* a good many things that an *honorable* man would not do.

There is undoubtedly a large territory of business relationships arising from modern methods of corporate enterprise which has not yet been fully surveyed and mapped in an ethical sense and this matter of "directors," or "inside" speculation falls partly in this territory. At present it is under a kind of provisional government with the principle *caveat emptor* as its main constitution. Perhaps some day the standard of strict *honesty* may more closely approximate the standard of *honor* than it now does. It is to be hoped that it will.

Summing up the lessons indicated as a result of our inquiry into stock speculation, we may recognize the existence of certain indubitable truths:

First: That probably most men who speculate do so without proper knowledge, and are really little better than gamblers in stocks.

Second: That most men who speculate in this way lose their money.

Third: That while speculation is a science, it is a most difficult science—all the more difficult because the very motive which leads most men to speculate is itself the fertile mother of most of their mistakes.

Fourth: Many of the principles upon which alone successful speculation can be based have their origin in the fact that the majority of those who buy and sell stocks speculatively always have been and probably always will be ignorant of the very existence of those principles—and

Lastly: Speculation in stocks cannot be prevented without serious economic consequences to the community, and no practicable method of wisely limiting it has ever been discovered.

The best way to prevent people who should not speculate from doing so is to educate them as to its dangers.

The Investment Digest

FOLLOWING is a list of publications, etc., from which this Digest is prepared. Where the name of a banking or brokerage house is given, the matter is taken from their special letter or circular: *Wall Street Journal; Boston News Bureau; Journal of Commerce;* N. Y. *Commercial;* N. Y. *Evening Mail;* N. Y. *Evening Post;* Com. and Fin. *Chronicle; Financial World; Railway World; U. S. Investor; Wall Street Summary; Commercial West;* Hayden, Stone & Co.; John Moody's Letter; Eugene Meyer, Jr., & Co.; Thomas Gibson's Letter; J. S. Bache & Co.'s Weekly Fin. Review; W. C. Langley & Co.; Wrenn Bros. & Co.; *Boston Commercial;* Robert Goodbody & Co.; *Moody's Magazine;* London *Statist;* Swartwout & Appenzellar; Kissel, Kinnicutt & Co.; Alfred Mestre & Co.; N. Y. *Evening Sun;* N. Y. *Times; Moody's Manual;* N. Y. *Journal;* N. Y. *Morning Sun; Financial Age;* N. Y. *World; Travel Magazine; Boston Post; Leslie's Weekly; Brooklyn Eagle; Kansas City Journal;* N. Y. *Herald;* N. Y. *Tribune; The Financial Record; Railroad Age Gazette;* Clement, Parker & Co. Neither THE TICKER nor the above authorities guarantee the information, but it is from sources considered trustworthy.

Allis Chalmers.—Report showed total earn. for the yr. of $1,809,009, and an inc. in work. cap. of $1,008.008, bringing the amt. up to $8,715,640.——The co. for several yrs. has been going through a proc. of upbuilding and it is prob. that in the cur. fisc. yr. will show what it is capable of doing in the matter of earn. That the co. starts its cur. fisc. yr. under fav. con. is evident from the fact that this mo. promises to establish a new high rec. in orders. Pres. says that for the three mos. of the cur. fisc. yr. the co.'s exp. of heavy vol. of biz. have been realized to the ext. of a reg. inc. in amt. each mo. In Sept. the total amt. of biz. booked exc. every mo. but one, since org. of the co.; and for the present mo. there is an equally large prosp.——Int. in Allis-Chal. affairs have recd. despatches from Cin. stating that the electrical business of the co. has reached so large a vol. that it has been decided to make exten. add. to the elec. plant in that city.

Am. Cotton Oil.—The net work. cap. of the co. on Aug. 31 was $7,565,375, of which $1,569.148 was cash in banks and $5,996.227 was bills and accts. receiv., marketable prod., raw mat. and supplies, after ded. cur. liab. The prof. shown for the yr. are the largest ever rec. in the co.'s history. The bal. sheet shows that the profit and loss surp. of the co. on Aug. 31 last was $9,255,-234, as comp. with $8,226,550 at the close of the prev. fisc. yr. Total quick assets of the co. on Aug. 31 last were $10,145,781 and cur. liab. $2,580,407. The co. had no bills payable, as comp. with bills and accts. receiv. and adv. for merch. of more than $4,000,000. ——The 5 p. c. com. stk. div. by Am. Cotton Oil, an inc. of 2 p. c., had been exp. The co. has distrib. its com. div. in one an. paymt. shortly after the close of the fisc. yr., Aug. 31. A yr. ago 4 p. c. was declared, of which 3 p. c. applied to '08 and 1 p. c. was on acct. of '07, when no distrib. was made. In '06, 2 p. c. was paid on the com. and, for two yrs. before that, but 1 p.

c. each yr. The present decl. is the largest since '02, when 6.p. c. was paid.

Am. Car & Foundry.—A director of the co. says: "The exp. has happened in r. r. equip. The flood of orders which poured in during Oct. seems likely to swamp us with work for mos. to come. The recov. in car equip. in gen. is attested by the statement that cars ordered or placed in Oct. were 50 p. c. of the amt. booked during the prec. nine mos. Up to Oct. 1 the r. r. had placed orders for approx. 100,000 new cars. Oct. orders for which cont. were signed or agreed to, were 45,000 cars, a total so far for the yr. of 145,000 new cars. This is consid. more than double the 63,000 cars ordered in all of '08, and very close to the '07 rec. of 152,000 cars for 12 mos. The co. is now running plants at full cap., and with biz. in hand is likely to find itself short of manuf. cap. in the near future. Am. Car & F. is free from any fin. prob. and well supplied with work. cap. For this reason an inc. in the com. div. to 4 p. c., against 2 p. c. now being paid, is hardly likely to be postp. beyond the close of the fisc. yr., Apr. 30 next.

Atlantic Coast Line.—The co. has called the reg. an. meeting for Nov. 16. At this meeting there will be subm. a prop. for auth. the issue of gold bonds not to exc. $200,000,000, bearing int. at not more than 4 p. c., and mat. at such dates as may be det. Part of the bonds are to be used for the retiremt. of the underlying mtge. bonds of the co., and for the retiremt. by exch. of its 4 p. c. certif. of indebt., not exc. $23,-562,500, and part for new const., imp. and other purposes.

Am. Beet Sugar.—The sugar-making season of the co. is now in full swing. Prod. began in Cal. early in Aug., with an output of 10.000 bags per day, and the Col. plants have just started slicing this mo. The prob. are that Am. Beet Sugar will make from 20 to 25 p. c. more sugar this yr. than last. The '08-'09 prod. was cut down by prolonged drought in Col., which lessened the yield of that state by 55 to 60 p. c. So far this year weather con. have been fav. for the slicing of a good-sized crop. The co. entered the '08-'09 selling season with a carry-over of 300,000 bags of sugar, so that in spite of its lessened prod. the co. last yr. was able to make the best showing of net in its history. This yr. the co. has a carry-over 66 p. c. less, or but 100,000 bags, but with the prac. assured inc. in prod., its total sales this yr. are likely to reach the normal fig. of about 130,000,000 lbs. Am. Beet Sugar now has an acreage under cul. upon which it can draw, of 52,000 acres beets. The co. is exp. this yr. in prop. imp. and ext. approx. $500,000, all of which will be paid for out of surp. earn. There are in the U. S. today 64 beet sugar factories, drawing on 450,000 acres of land and slicing 4,564,000 tons of beets. The three leading beet sugar states are Col., Mich. and Cal.

Am. Locomotive.—The biz. of the co. has begun to assume a large vol. which has forced it materially to inc. oper. at its plants. The railroad buying of loco. has begun to fill the predictions made earlier in the yr. Some of the larger orders just placed with the co. are for 267 loco. from the N. Y. C., 100 from the Chic. & Northw., for deliv. next yr., and 50 from the St. Paul.

Am. Malting.—Chairman Sully concl. as follows: "Attention of st'kholders is again called to the plan for red. and readj. of cap. and to the fact that of a total of 289,-400 shs. of pfd. and com. stk., 268,826 shs. have been dep. under the said plan and exch. for stks. of the Am. Malt Corp., leaving less than 3.31 p. c. of the cap. stk. of the Am. Malting Co. in the hands of the public unassented. It should again be said that no adv. can be gained by outst. shareholders of the Am. Malting Co. in withholding assent to the above plan and there are very obv. adv. to each class of stk. in making the exch." The bal. sheet showed a prof. and loss surp. on Aug. 31 last of $980,207, against $1,430,735 in the yr. prev. There was an inc. in cash on hand and in banks of approx. $1,400,000, as comp. with the prev. yr.

Amalgamated.—Boston & Mon. is prod. over 100,000,000 lbs. of copper at approx. 9 cents per lb. On 13-cent copper, cur. prof. should be at the rate of $4,000,000 per an., a sum eq. to $2.65 per sh. on the entire cap. stk. of the Amal. Co. It is apparent that Boston & Mon. is today more than earn. the $2 div. now paid to Amal. st'kholders. There are 150,000 shs. of Boston & Mont., and with the exc. of a few shs. it is owned in its entirety by the Amalgamated. Anaconda is doing about 90,-000,000 lbs., and something over one-half of this output accrues to the Amal. Anaconda is making a cost of a little over 10 cents per lb.; is earn. better than $2.25 per sh., and is paying div. of $2 per an. The anomaly is presented of Amal. selling at

78 and paying $2 in divs., while Anaconda, paying same div., sells for only 46.——The Butte & Boston Co., prac. all of whose 200,000 shs. are in the treas. of the Amal. Co., is making the best record of earns. in its career. An Amal. official is quo. as saying that the Butte & Boston Co. for the first six mos. of this yr. had prod. at the rate of 20,000,000 lbs. of copper per an., at a cost of not over 10 cents per lb.

Am. Hide & Leather.—The pfd. stk. of this co. remains neglected despite the much imp. cond. in its affairs. Not only is the co. earn. close to 10 p. c. on the stk., on which over 66 p. c. in back divs. have accumulated, but hides are bringing higher prices notwithst. the tariff red. This means add. profits. Am. Hide & Leather pfd. is selling close to Cent. Leather com. while it is intrin. worth 100 p. c. more.

Am. Tel. & Tel.—The auth. cap. stk. of Am. Tel. is $300,000,000, of which $22,000,-000 has for yrs. been res. in the treas. At present the co. has over $250,000,000 stock outst. and at least $40,000,000 more must be res. for the con. of the approx. $60,000,000 bonds not yet conv. into stk. Here is a total of $312,000,000 stk., so that it is ap. that Am. Tel., to effect the N. Y. Tel. Co. merger, must have dipped into its treas. stk., which, by the way, is a remnant of the 1900 merger when the Am. Tel. absorbed the Am. Bell Tel. Co.

Am. Steel Foundries.—The an. rept. of the co., to July 31, 1909, will show a striking inc. over '08. The nine plants of the co. are running on full time and are fairly swamped with orders. During period of dep., when work was susp. in several plants, neces. add. and imp. were made and with the ever inc. vol. of biz. the '10 yr. should be one of the best in its history.

Atchison, Topeka & S. F.—It will be noted that of the $25,900,000 inc. in gross earns., $8,700,000 were saved for com. stk.; conseq'tly, while gross earns. inc. 38 p. c., the bal. app. to divs. on the com. incd. 140 p. c. The co.'s recup. power is another point in its favor. In one yr. after one of the most severe biz. dep., both gross and net earns. ret. to practically the level of its former most prosp. yr.; thus, all gains in the cur. yr. over '09 carry the co. into new ground. The conserv. of the management in decl. divs. is also app. Of the $56,000,000 surp. earned in these five yrs., less than one-half, $25,300,000, was distrib. to com. st'kholders, the bal. of $30,700,000 being applied in some way to the upbuild. of the prop. The bal. sheet, as of June 30, '09, reveals a very strong position in the matter of work. cap. The yr.'s outlay, over and above ord. maint. chgs., was almost entirely cov. by approp. from inc., leaving the co. at close of the yr. with $30,000,000 cash. Excl. of mat. and supplies, it now has a work. cap. of $18,000,000, to which must be added the $30,000,000 to be recd. from the new issue of conv. bonds, making a total of $48,000,000 wherewith to carry on the biz. and throw out new lines into unoccupied ter.——Atchison's gross and net earns. in the three mos. to Sept. 30, '09, were the greatest ever rep. by the road in that quar. Gross amtd. to $25,434,-886, an inc. over the prev. record for the period, estab. in 1907, of $1,429,322. Net likewise was over $1,000,000 better than ever earned in the same three mos. before.

Am. Woolen.—The rumor has gained circulation that Am. Woolen was to take some action in com. stk. divs. after the turn of the yr. The weight of sentiment still contin. strongly opp. to any distrib. of surp. earns. for com. divs. Ever since the co. was formed there has been pressure from one quar. or another for com. div. action, but this the managemt. has always been successful in resisting. As developments have shown, this policy has been the main factor contrib. to the perm. of the 7 p. c. pfd. div. rate.

Baltimore & Ohio.—It will cost Balt. & Ohio approx. $21,000,000 to obtain control of Chic. Term. Trans. Co. To the Chic., Burl. & Q. the co. will have to pay about $5,500,000 to secure about $16,000,000 par val. of Term. stk. from the Hill people. Chic. advices state that paymt. is to be made in 4 p. c. short-term notes.——The an. report for yr. end. June 30 shows gross earn. of $71,043,519, against $73,608,-781, and net earns. of $23,491,976, as comp. with $19,457,902 in the prev. yr. Oper. exp. suffered a consid. reduc., being $47,551,976 against $54,150,978 in '08, leaving bal. avail. for divs. on the com. stk. of $10,072,981, which was eq. to 6.9 p. c. earned, against 5.1 p. c. earned in the prev. yr.

Bethlehem Steel.—At a special meeting Bethlehem Steel shareholders, the management of the co. was auth. to pledge any part of the stks. of subsid. cos. as col. for an issue of $7,500,000 6 p. c. five-yr. notes. Proceeds from the sale of the notes are to be used to take up $2,500,000 6 p. c. mat. notes, and to pay for imp. designed to inc. the co.'s cap.——At special meeting of the Beth. Steel Corp., a st'kholder questioned Pres. Schwab as to the prob. of a div. on the com. stk. Mr. Schwab stated that he could not hold out hope for resump. of com. divs., at least not during next yr. In expl., stated that while the plants were oper. at full cap., at the same time consid. had to be taken of the fact that personal funds had been adv. to supply floating cap. and other necess. of the co., and until these funds had been retd., he did not think it would be proper to take up the question of com. divs. For the pres., Mr. Schwab said, his chief int. lay in paying divs. on the pfd. He added that he himself was drawing no salary as pres. of the co.

Brooklyn Rap. Transit.—Pub. Service Com. makes public report for period of 3 mos. end. June 30th, as follows: Gross earns., $5,258,125; oper. exp., $3,480,663; net earns., $1,777,462; other inc., $121,493; total inc., $1,898,955; taxes, $313,829; int., $933,-727; rentals, $397,125; other chgs., $1,400; total chgs., $1,646,081; net inc., $252,874.

Butterick Co.—The prop. inc. in the cap. stk. from $12,000,000 to $15,000,000 is for the purpose of taking over the Ridgway Pub. Co., publish. of "Everybody's Mag." By the terms of the deal, three shs. of Butterick will be given for one sh. of Ridgway. The Ridgway Co. is capitalized at $1,000,-000, and the $3,000,000 inc. will be used entirely for the pur. The Butterick Co. is paying divs. of 2 p. c. per an. While no figures can be obtained, it is claimed that Ridgway is earning enough to pay the 2 p. c. rate on the $3,000,000 add. stk., which amts. to $60,000 and leave a good surp.

Canadian Pacific.—Only part of the $20,-000,000 which Can. Pac. gets for the 995,-000 acres sold this fisc. yr. out of the "western block" has been paid for in cash, the bal. being in 5 p. c. and 6 p. c. notes. An. int. on the bal. rep. by these notes alone will make up about two-thirds of the 1 p. c. div. on the $10,000,000 com. stk. which is yrly. paid out of int. rec. on land sale bal.

Central Leather.—The transf. of U. S. Leather shs. to the Cent. Co. at the 130 fig. recently nego. for the Colgate int., is about compl. After the first lot of 30,000 shs. had been exch. on the above terms there remained 10,000 still outst. The Colgate firm suc. in bringing together almost the entire amt., and the shs. still out are mainly in the hands of indiv. who have been away and unable to send in the sec. quickly. The Cent. Co. is expected to have the exch. comp. before the directors meet next.

Chesapeake & Ohio.—Co. reports for Sept. an inc. in surp. earns. of $211,163. For the first quar. the inc. was $524,466, or 46 p. c. If this rate of inc. is main., the stk. would show earn. this year at the rate of 9.3 p. c.

Chgo., Burlington & Quincy.—A Bur. official says: "Our traffic is incg. and we are hard pressed for cars. Misc. and merch. tonnage is very heavy, the movement of grain fair and coal shipmts. have imp. About 80 p. c. of the mine capacity in our ter. is working. Sept. biz. was 10 p. c. better than a yr. ago, and also exc. the same time in 1907." Report states that cap. stk. of the co. remained unch. on June 30 last, but the funded debt was inc. by $20,309,000 to $203,373,000. Expend. for const. during the yr. amted. to $1,412,744. The total amt. at the credit of sinking funds on June 30, '08, was $29,127,441, which amt. was inc. by $1,134,824 during the late fisc. period. Pres. says that there is reason for believing that the pur. of the Col. & So. by the Burl. during the yr. will prove beneficial to both int. The bal. sheet, as of June 30 last, shows cash on hand amtg. to $15,064,572; mat. and supplies, $5,-882,191; sundry invts., $11,073,130, and a profit and loss surp. of $14,187,325.

Chgo., Cin. & Louisville.—In regard to recent pur. by Newman Erb, of $2,600,000 of the $3,100,000 2d mtge. bonds, it may be def. stated on high auth. that Mr. Hawley is entirely in cont. of Chic., Cin. & Louisv.

Mr. Erb acted in the int. of Mr. Hawley, with whom he had a friendly underst. in purch. the bonds.

Chgo. & Eastern Ill.—The pamphlet report for the fisc. yr. end. June 30 last states: The bal. sheet shows cash on hand, $947,967, contrasted with $646,448 the prev. yr.; total cur. assets of $7,552,889, against $9,621,038; cur. liab., $3,889,250, as against $5,159,775. and prov. accts. of $1,410,259, as comp. with $1,203,625 in 1908.

Chgo., Milwaukee & St. Paul.—Facing the necessity of earning $3,750,000 more after chgs. in 1909-10 than last yr. to meet its greater div. req., St. Paul is concen. its attention upon red. exp. The road is doing a good business—the commerce commission's fig. for July and Aug. show a gain of $777,588 in gross. But oper. exp., excl. taxes, have inc. in that time $1,273,493, or 20 p. c., leaving a dec. of $495,905 in net op. inc. The St. Paul Puget Sound exten. earn. are reported at the rate of $6,000,000 per an. above the oper. exp.——The co. has sold to the Nat. City Bank and Kuhn, Loeb & Co. $3,000,000 add. 4 p. c. deb. gold bonds, making total of $28,000,000 now sold and outst. out of an auth. issue of $50,000,000. The $28,000,000 now sold and outst. are to be listed on the N. Y. Stock Exch. at once. App. has been made to the N. Y. Stock Exch. to list $50,000,000 25-yr. 4 p. c. deb. of 1934.

Chgo. & Northwestern.—Directors of the co. will meet in a few days to auth. offering to st'kholders add. stk.; at par, equal to 15 p. c. of their present holdings. As the co. has outst. $124,351,685 com. and pfd. stk., this is equiv. to an issuance of about $18,500,000 new stk. at par, and gives shareholders rights roughly est. at bet. $11 and $12.

Cincinnati, Ham. & Dayton.—Bankers have concl. neg. covering $12,500,000 1st and ref. mtge. 50-year 4 p. c. gold bonds. These bonds are guar. by the Balt. & Ohio. ——These bonds are part of a total auth. issue of $75,000,000. The pro. of the present issue will be used as follows: $5,500,000 for the paymt. or adj. of indebt. of the co. both due and acc., $5,000,000 for imp. and $2,000,000 for work. cap. Of the same class of bonds, $13,000,000 are issued for dep. as col. under the 4 p. c. notes due July 1, 1913, making $27,500,000 in all outst. under the first and ref. mtge.; and $47,500,000 held in res. for future use, $23,714,000 of which will be used for add. and betterments and $23,786,000 for ref. underlying bonds.

Corn Products.—The co. is grinding over 100,000 bush. of corn a day and is oper. at full cap. While earns. show material imp., it is not believed inc. for cur. fisc. yr. will be suf. to justify more than 5 p. c. on the pfd. stk.

Colorado Fuel & Iron.—Standard Oil people have now full con. of prop. and owning most of the stk. and bonds, they will make out of the prop. a big success. J. D. Rockefeller himself has decl. that he has put one of his best men into the management to make Col. Fuel a big thing.—— Earns. of the co. at the present time, both gross and net, are the largest in the history of the corp. Net prof. for the fisc. yr. end. June 30 made a new high rec., with a total of $3,346,772, or $858,375 for the com. after int. and other chgs. Ints. close to the managemt. state that at present net prof. are running at rate to show $10 per sh. for the $34,235,500 com., against $2.40 per sh. in the fisc. twelve mos. just ended. Co. is equipped to prod. 750,000 tons of manuf. steel per an., and if present biz. is maint. for a mo. or two longer, the full cap. will be called upon for the current fisc. yr. The expert managemt. now assured, C. F. & I. com. is one of the cheapest steel sec. in the entire list and has not yet begun to disc. the prosp. in store. It is believed that the acc. divs. on the pfd., of which there is but $2,000,000 outst., will shortly be adj. either by the ret. of that issue or the paymt. of the back divs. in full.

Colorado & Southern.—The full pamph. report shows effect of Burl. control. This co. has been remark. for its contin. gain in the '08 fisc. yr. This gain was contin. during the past twelve mos., the co. rep. largest gross earns. in its history, but this inc. was largely taken up by heavier oper. exp., leaving the surp. at about the same fig. as for the last two yrs. With gross inc. of only $15,000,000, Co. is exp. over $1,100,000 a yr. more in main. than it was three yrs. ago. This is not a policy that is cond. to large spec. adv., but counts in the long run.

Consolidated Gas.—With gross oper. rev., slightly in excess of $12,000,000 for the 12 mos. end. Dec. 31, 1908, the Co. recorded a bal. avail. for divs. equal to 4.07 p. c. on the $99,454,500 outst. cap. stk. The bal. sheet of the co., as of Dec. 31, 1908, showed an excep. inc. in cash over the corres. date of the yr. prev.—$5,881,082—the amt. on hand being $6,380,698.

Copper Metal.—Rumors of a combination of one group of Copper producers and a Gentleman's Agreement with another for the purpose of limiting the output of copper in America to the demands of the trade, and to enable producers to realize a profitable return, are so persistent that we call attention to a few copper stocks the price of which should be favorably affected by such a combination.

The bulk of the copper output of the country is controlled by six groups, as follows:

Amalgamated, Cole-Ryan, output per annum, 500,000,000 pounds, controls the Amalgamated, Anaconda, Parrott, Utah Cons., International Smelting & Refining Co., Butte Coalition, Calumet & Arizona and Superior & Pittsburg; Giroux, Greene Cananea, North Butte.

Guggenheim Exploration Co., production 250,000,000 pounds, controls the American Smelting & Refining Co., controlling First National, Nevada Cons., and Cumberland Ely, Utah Copper, Ray Cons. and others.

Phelps-Dodge & Co., output 180,000,000 pounds, controls the Copper Queen, Detroit, Montezuma, Old Dominion. Treats custom ores and sells copper produced by Calumet & Arizona, Superior & Pittsburg and others.

Calumet & Hecla, production 130,000,000 pounds, controls the Calumet & Hecla, Centennial, La Salle, Osceola, Superior, Isle Royale, Ahmeek, Tamarack.

American Metal controls 150,000,000 pounds; L. Vogelstein & Co., 100,000,000 pounds; miscellaneous, 90,000,000 pounds; total annual, 1,400,000,000 pounds.

Denver & Rio Grande.—N. Y. Stock Exch. has listed $5,011,000 additional first and ref. mtge. 5 p. c. bonds, due in 1955, making total amt. listed $27,944,000.——At the an. meeting of the st'kholders held Oct. 19, the action of the old board in giving a $150,000,000 mtge. to prov. a res. fund, take up outst. bonds, assist in finan. the Western Pac., and for gen. corp. exp., was ratified. ——The Western Pac., when compl. and in oper., will virtually be an exten. of the Denver & Rio G. system, and it will not only furnish a Pac. coast outlet for this co., but for the Mo. Pac. and affiliated lines as well. These roads have an agg. of about 18,000 miles, not counting those cos. having traffic ar. with the D. & R. G. and subsidiaries, and which will contrib. to the traf. rev. of this Pac. coast exten. The fin. of the road up to the point of oper. is now prac. comp. Its cap. acct. consists of stk. to the auth. and issued amt. of $75,-000,000. Two-thirds of this cap. stk., or about $50,000,000, is in the treas. of the D. & R. G. There is auth. and issued $50,000,-000 first mtge. 5 p. c. bonds, and of an auth. amt. of $25,000,000 second mtge. 5 p. c. bonds about $23,230,000 were issued to the D. & R. G. in consid. of funds furnished by the parent co. in financing building oper.

Distillers.—The report for the yr. end. June 30 shows a net profit of nearly $400,-000. The co. is still struggling against the Prohibition wave, and drastic econ. have been carried on. The bal. sheet shows gross profits of only $2,683,236, as against $2,454,930 in the very bad year of '08. The net profit is equal to 2.26 p. c. on the $32,-478,400 cap. stk.

Erie.—Erie's gross earns. in Sept. ran ahead of those for Sept., 1908, by $482,000, or at the rate of $5,775,000 a yr. It was an inc. of about 11 p. c., and is the most encouraging sign of recovery Erie has rep. in many mos. An inc. in gross traf. earns. is more to the road's credit than an adv. in the amt. of the net, if the latter has to be obtained by red. exp.

Great Northern.—The pamphlet report for fisc. yr. end. June 30 shows the balance avail. for divs. equal to 8.32 p. c. on the $209,970,250 stk. outst. on June 30 last, as comp. with 7.13 p. c. earned on the $209,-962,750 stk. outst. on June 30, '08. The bal. sheet shows cash on hand $9,144,105, as comp. with $11,688,302 on June 30, '08; to-

tal cur. assets of $16,049,949, contrasted with $19,913,782; mat. and fuel on hand, $6,354,215, against $8,219,580; cur. liab., $7,-539,021, comp. with $7,042,481 and a profit and loss surp. of $35,146,545, against $27,-191,800 in the prev. yr. On June 30 land owned by the co. unsold was 815,461 acres. During the yr. 3,637 acres were sold at an avge. of $9.99 per acre.

Inter. Steam Pump.—The N. Y. Stock Exch. has listed $8,500,000 temp. first lien 25-yr. 5 p. c. sinking fund bonds of the co.

Interb. Rap. Transit.—The Pub. Serv. Com. has made public a statement from the quar. report, cover. the period of 3 mos. end. June 30. Gross earn. from oper., $6,-816,850; oper. exp., $2,656,315; net earn., $4,-160,535; other inc., $343,210; total inc., $4,-503,745; taxes, $454,764; int., $501,261; rentals, $2,004,535; other chgs., $3,036; total chgs., $2,963,596; net inc., $1,540,149.

Inter. Harvester.—The biz. of the co., so far this yr., has been better than ever before, and this imp. has been marked in export as well as dom. trade. This co. is one of the best managed indus. corp., and there is an esprit de corps among empl., owing to the fact that they are large st'kholders to an ext. prob. eq. only by the Steel Corp. The co. and the Steel Corp. are closely con., as E. H. Gary, N. B. Ream, Charles Steele and G. W. Perkins are directors of both, and all steel req. for harvest. mach. is purch. from the Steel Corp.

International Paper.—The report of oper. for yr. end. June 30, has just been issued. Gross earn. were $18,238,476, as comp. with $20,716,304 in the prev. yr. Op. exp. were $16,456,379, as comp. with $17,878,134, and net earns. were $1,782,097, as against $2,-838,170 in 1908. Int. taxes and insur. used up $1,183,995 of this amt., leaving a bal. of $598,102 avail. for divs., which was equal to 2.66 p. c. earned on the pfd. stk., and comp. with 7.39 p. c. earned in the prev. yr.

Illinois Central.—The New York Stock Exch. has listed $12,000,000 pur. lines first mtge. 3½ p. c. bonds, due 1952.

Kansas City Southern.—Arrangemts. have been made to pay off $5,100,000 col. gold notes, and to make consid. imp. in term., for which purposes $10,000,000 ref. and imp. bonds were auth. July 1, '09. The bal. sheet shows cur. assets of $2,798,993 and cur. liab. of $2,040,911. Cash on hand June 30 was $1,564,348, not incl. $5,100,000 res. for redemption of notes outst. The total profit and loss bal. was $3,863,208, a gain of $713,499.

Louisville & Nashville.—When the stk. prev. sold around this level in '05 and '06, the best showing the co. ever made was over 11 p. c. In the fisc. yr. end. June 30, '09, it earn. over 14¼ p. c., or nearly twice earned in '08. In the two mos. end. Aug., '09, there was a gain in gross of $569,000, of which $518,000 were saved for net. At this rate the bal. of yr., L. & N. will earn net $11,000,000, or 18 p. c. on its $60,000,000. The co. is one of the very few which have made no large add. to their cap., the $60,-

000,000 stk. remaining the same since '05, while since that time there has been an inc. in the fund. debt of only $22,000,000; consequently, every actual inc. in net earns. is refl. in a corres. inc. in the perct. earned on cap. In matter of ratio between earn. and market price, L. & N. shows up the best of any of the larger systems, except only Atch.

Minneapolis, St. Paul and S. Ste. M.— N. Y. Stock Exch. has listed on and after Oct. 15, '09, $2,016,000 add. pfd. stk. and $4,032,000 add. com., on notice of issuance and paymt. in full, making total amt. auth. to be listed $10,416,000 pfd. and $20,832,000 com. stk.

Missouri, Kansas & Texas.— Mo., K. & T. has demon. its ability to main. the 4 p. c. div. on its $13,000,000 pfd. through good times and poor; in yrs. of abund., such as '07, it earned as high as 5¼ p. c. on its $63,300,000 com., comp. with less than ½ p. c. last yr. and less than 1 p. c. for the fisc. yr. just concl. The prop. has been well main. and the policy of the managemt. has been to spend about $2,000,000 per yr. on new const., half of which has been taken from earn. About $4,500,000 has been thus exp. in the past four yrs.——At present price of nearly $50, the com. shs. may be said to have disc. earn. of 5 p. c., and prosp. do not favor a return to 5 p. c. earn. for some time. For fisc. yr. to end June 30, '10, earn. for the com., from pres. indic., will not much exceed 3 p. c., although it must be recog. that the Mo., K. & T. has a more rap. growing ter. than any other of the so-called Hawley roads.

Northern Pacific.— The co. earned last yr. 8.72 p. c. on its $248,000,000 of cap. stk., which comp. fav. with 8.02 p. c. earned in '08 on the same basis of cap. The oper. rev. for the yr. is $68,461,747, all deptmts., except the pass. dept., showing subst. inc. The net oper. inc. was $30,020,005, an inc. of $2,060,749, and the net bal. app. to divs. after all deduc., was $21,639,380, an inc. of $1,746,283, compared with the prev. yr. Divs. amtg. to $14,105,000 were paid, as comp. with $10,850,000 in '08.

Norfolk & Western.— Decl. div. of 2½ p. c., comp. with 2 p. c. paid last June, now placed on 5 p. c. div. basis.——Co. makes a new record for Sept., showing a surp. avail. for divs. of $854,663. The surp. for the first quar. of the fisc. yr. was $2,189,294, or at the rate of 4 p. c. per an. on the pfd. stk. and 12 p. c. on the com.

North American.— For fisc. yr. end. Dec. 31, '08, the co. earned 4.86 p. c. on the outstanding stock of $29,793,300. In April of the pres. yr. divs. were renewed. The stk. is now on a 5 p. c. basis. Notwithstanding better biz. outlook and inc. in earn., it is not exp. that there will be an inc. in the rate. That the co. will earn at least 5 p. c. on its stk. this yr. is certain.

N. Y. Air Brake.— The co. has been awarded the contract by the N. Y. Cent. to equip the 325 loco., 197 pass. cars and 17,850 freight cars, which are to be built

the coming yr. The total equip. will cost $25,000,000, and of that amt. over $1,000,000 will go to the N. Y. Air Brake Co. for brakes.——The co. is planning to resume divs. on the $13,000,000 cap. stk. sometime after Jan. It is prob. that the rate will be 6 p. c. instead of 8 p. c., as was paid for a number of yrs. The co. has been out of the list of div.-payers since Oct., '07. The rush of equip. orders has filled the co.'s plants with work, and the Watertown, N. Y., plant is now booked several mos. ahead of full cap.

N. Y. Central.— Pres. Brown says: "Traffic in Sept. and Oct. to date exc. anything in our history. Every avail. car and engine is in service; 94 p. c. of freight cars are in use, the remaining 6 p. c. being in repair shops. We could do 10 p. c. more biz. if we had the equip."——Co. has placed con. during the past few days for new equip. for deliv. during '10, involv. about $25,000,000. These incl. 325 locos., 197 pass. cars and 17,850 freight cars. Cont. are also being arranged for 165,000 tons of rails for '10 delivery, which will involve about $4,620,000.——The N. Y. Cent. has applied to the Pub. Serv. Com. for auth. to issue $44,658,000 add. stk. Acc. to the app. filed, part of the pro. of the sale of the new stk. will be used to ret. $25,000,000 5 p. c. gold notes mat. Feb. 1, '10, and the bal. will go toward various imp. projects.

N. Y., New Haven & Hartford.— The saving in transp. costs, as comp. with former basis, is equiv. to $2,000,000, or an an. ret. of 4 p. c. on the above exp. In add. the road has been enabled, by the incd. facilities created, to carry a much larger vol. of gross biz. The incd. cap. may be meas. by $10,000,000 add. gross, or from $50,000,000 to $60,000,000 total. This added gross gives $3,000,000 add. net, which is equiv. to another 6 p. c. on the above total expend. This makes a total of 10 p. c. ret. on money exp. for railroad imp.——At a special meeting, it was unan. voted to inc. the cap. stk. by $50,000,000, making $171,000,000 of stk. auth. Pres. Mellen said that its 8 p. c. divs. are better sec. today than ever. All of the new stk. is to be issued at once and paid for in four semi-an. instal. at 125.

Pacific Coast Co.— The action this week in adv. div. on the $11,000,000 second pfd. and com. from 4 to 5 p. c. will be followed by a second inc. in Jan. to 6 p. c., thus restoring the full rate in force up to the time of the panic. There was no good reason for withholding the full inc. at this week's decl., but the board desired to be conserv. Earn. are now back to normal. For quar. end. Sept. 30 the inc. in net was over 100 p. c., comp. with same period of a yr. ago. Expend. for prop. add. this cur. fisc. yr. will be very light and $200,000 of exp. on this acct. would be an outside fig.

People's Gas.— Gross and net earn. for the yr. to end Dec. 31 will estab. new high rec. if the co. during the remain. 2½ mos. does not more than equal '08 showing for this period. Gross sales of $14,500,000 with a bal. for divs. of over 9 p. c. on $35,000,000 stk., or $2,000,000 more than was outst. during the '08 fisc. 12 mos., are exp. In spite of pres. rec. earns., any inc. above the 7 p. c. rate is unlikely. The co. has import. fran. ques. to settle with the city of Chic. in Feb., 1911, and a higher rate than 7 p. c. would prob. be an invi. for a still further reduc. in gas prices.

Pennsylvania.—Penn. lines east of Pittsb. and Erie, directly oper., show inc. in gross rev. for mo. of Sept. of $1,755,300 and an inc. in net of $942,000. For the nine mos. end. Sept. 30 gross inc. $11,409,000, and net inc. $4,113,800. Lines west of Pittsb. and Erie directly oper. show an inc. in gross earn. for Sept. of $1,826,500, and an inc. in net of $867,400. Nine mos. gross inc. $9,222,500 and net inc. $2,847,000.—— The holders of the Penn. conv. 3½s of 1912 can conv. into stk., at the holders' option, at $70 per sh. at any time. The bonds are subj. to redemp. at 102½ on 90 days' notice. The conv. 3½s of '15 are conv. into stk. at $75 per sh. at option of holder, and they are subj. to redemp. at par and int. on Dec. 1, '10, and at any subsequent int. date on 90 days' notice, but, if called, the holder may still exercise the conv. priv.——Details of the new $80,000,000 stk. issue. Holders of rec. Nov. 15 will be per. to subs. to the ext. of 25 p. c. of their holdings at par from Dec. 8 to Dec. 18, on which date the priv. will cease. Payments may be made in full at time of subscription or in three instal. Th first, of 30 p. c., or $15 per sh., at time of making the subscp.; the second, of 30 p. c., bet. Feb. 23 and Mar. 1, '10, incl., and third, of 40 p. c., or $20 per sh., bet. May 26 and June 1, '10, incl.——The vast amt. of improvement and const. work now compl. will enable the Penn. to handle inc. of traffic. No new fin. is contemp. next yr. It has taken several yrs. to carry out the imp. work; and now, instead of its sec. being dep. by large cap. issues, the prosp. is that their position and earn. power will be strengthened by the const. coming into productivity. The climax of Penn.'s achievts. will come in June next with the opening to the pub. of the greatest of all term., giving the system direct ent. into N. Y. Cy. If the term. opening is prec. by an inc. div. decl. in May, there will be fur. a doubly striking impression of the value of Penn. stk. Earn. for yr. '09 are at the rate of 11 p. c. per an. Indic. are that by next May they will be at the rate of 12 p. c. Ample basis for an inc. div. will be afforded.

Pittsburg Coal.—Three yrs. ago the co. had a floating indebt. of $10,000,000. This has been wiped out and today the surplus in bank is greater than cur. liab. During same period the bonded indebt. has been dec. $6,000,000. Estim. by competent auth. the book value of the com. and pfd. is equiv. to 125 for each class of stk. The last rept. of the co. shows that it owns some 160 mines, which incl. 193,309 acres.——There

is a rumor that the pfd. div. accum., amtg. to 31½ p. c., are to be liq., that the coke holdings will be sold to U. S. Steel. The latter is the most val. holding the co. has and the outlook for the coke indus. is flattering. The co. will be rid of its floating indebt. by Jan. 1, and it is confid. exp. that a div. will be paid in April.

Pressed Steel Car.—More than 2,000 workmen have begun work. Orders to start the plant have been issued and final prep. for this made. The rush of car orders the past ten days has added more than 4,500 cars to the books of the co. which were already fairly well filled. There is yet to be heard from the Pressed Steel Co.'s portion of recent order of the Balti. & Ohio, which will run into some thousands of cars, and these are to be followed by other orders known to be auth. by railroad boards but not yet allotted.

Pullman.—Earn. on the $100,000,000 stk. for the fisc. yr. end. July 31, '09, were eq. to 14.7 p. c. before ded. dep. chges., and 10.9 p. c. after ded. $3,794,323 for this purp. Net earn., $14,742,525, show an inc. of $1,124,043, or 8.2 p. c. over '08. Bal. after divs. was $2,949,131, as comp. with $1,790,569 in '08, an inc. of $1,158,562, or 63.5 p. c. During the interv. of three yrs. since the co. paid its last stk div., it has earned and paid 8 p. c. on $26,000,000 add. stk., has chged. $10,794,817 to dep. and other ded., and has accum. a surp. of $9,995,918, eq. to nearly 10 p. c. on $100,000,000 cap. stk. outstanding at the. pres. time.——The co.'s books are rep. to be so well filled with cont. that it is seeking no new biz., and has enough work ahead to keep its plants fully occupied until next Aug.

Reading.—The feature of Sept. statemt. is the very heavy gross earn. of the railway co.—there is an inc. of $300,000 for the mo. and $1,000,000 for the first three mos. of the fisc. yr. The Coal & Iron Co. shows a def. for the mo. of $70,920, comp. with net of $154,438 in Sept., '08. Reading's prod. of coal in Sept. this yr. was but 845,000 tons, comp. with 1,040,000 in Sept., 1908. The Reading Co. inc. its net about $24,000 and surp. of the three cos. after fixed chgs. and taxes was $751,649, comp. with $774,414. Consid. the dec. in the anthra. ton., the result was very satisf. and again demonstrated the ability of the co. to earn money when the anthra. movem. is light.

Rock Island.—There are prom. feat. to the full report of the co., which appeared recently. Although an inc. in gross of $2,700,000, there was prac. no inc. in oper. exp., and at the same time the maint. exp. were consid. larger than those for the prev. yr., these being offset by a dec. in the cost of "con. transp." Not only did it recov. the loss in gross earns. of the prev. yr. of $1,650,000, but exc. the gross earns. of '07, rep. the largest gross oper. rev. in its history. But for maint. chgs. larger by $500,000, and an inc. in fixed chgs. of $1,500,000, the co. would have rep. the largest net in its history. This net was suffi. to pay the div. of 5¼ p. c., prac. all of which go to the holding co., and are suf. to defray the latter's fixed chgs., and show a surp. of $2,-236,000. The latter is eq. to a little over 4 p. c. on the pfd. stk. of the R. I. Co. The St. Lou. & San Fran. would show a surp. above its fixed chgs. of $2,500,000, and, after allowing for the divs. on its pfd. shs. the surp. for the com., or R. I.'s eq., would amt. to $1,660,000. This would make a total eq. behind the R. I. shs. of $5,400,000, equiv. to the full 5 p. c. divs. to which the pfd. stk. will be entitled next yr., and over 3 p. c. on the com.——"The co. is doing all the business it has equip. for," said an official of that system. "We have made steady inc. and are looking for traf. to continue up to the present level for some time. The distrib. of merch. is very large, and there is a decided inc. in the coal tonnage."

Sears Roebuck Co.—It is offi. stated that the co.'s surp. on July 1 last was $7,150,000, or an inc. of about $1,500,000 comp. with Jan. 1, '09. Results from the cur. 6 mos. are exp. to add a very large amt. to the above sum. Con. in the surp. are said to be $2,000,000 N. Y. Cy. bonds, misc. sec., and a large amt. of cash. In verifying these fig., Mr. Rosenwald stated that further inc. will be made in the div. rate on the com. stk., although when such incs. are made somethin gwould have to be carried to the surp. acct. He decl. that the distrib. of surp. on the junior shs. had always been ordered with the utmost conserv., and that this policy would be followed in the future.

Seaboard Air Line.—In the reorg., Judge Lacombe granted order directing that all recs.' indebt. be called for paymt. on Nov. 6, and that the prop. and biz. of the co. in hands of receivers be turned over to the co. on Nov. 4. The order directs the issuance of new sec. and bonds and the rec. of new mtgs. and agreemts. Also that all outst. certif. and other obli. of the rec. be adj. a lien on the prop. until paid. The court res. its right to renew poss. of the road if the indebt. is not paid. The recs.' certif. are to be paid by the Continental Trust Co. of Baltimore and Blair & Co., N. Y., and they are also in add. to pay $700,000 2-yr. 6 p. c. notes of the co., all overdue int., and first mtge. 4 p. c. bonds and such portion of the outst. notes amtg. to $2,488,583 with int.

Southern Railway.—The earnings of the So. Ry. are very signif. In the yr. end. June 30, '07, and again June 30, '08, this system earned only $300,000 over fixed chges. But in the yr. end. June 30, '09, it earned $3,500,000 in exc. of such chgs. Since July 1 it has gained about $500,000 a mo. over the big inc. of last yr. and for the first wk. in Oct. it rep. an inc. in gross of $166,000. ——The an. report shows almost 6 p. c. earned for the pfd. stk. The system is in the fav. position of being able to largely inc. its gross earn., and, at the same time, to handle its biz. at a red. ratio of oper.

St. Louis Southwestern.—Reports for July and Aug. show an inc. of 53 p. c., in oper. inc. This ind. 7.7 p. c. earngs. on the pfd. stk., which comp. with 3 p. c. for the last fisc. yr., and an avge. of 4 p c. for the last five yrs. But as the recent inc. was largely due to red. in exp., it is doubtful whether it can be maint.

St. Louis & San. Fran.—N. Y. Stock Exch. has listed $1,022,000 add. 4 p. c. ref. mtge. bonds, due 1951, making total amt. listed $67,022,000.——Co. repts. for last yr. a surp. of $1,328,586, which comp. with $459,067 in '07-'08, and $4,158,583 in '06-'07. As the full 4 p. c. div. on the 1st pfd. req. only $199,742, and the full 4 p. c. on the non-cumu. 2nd pfd., which was discon. in '06, req. only $640,000, it is evi. that the com. stk., all of which is owned by R. I. and pledged for their 5 p. c. col. tr. bonds, has great possib.——James Speyer placed in Germany $6,000,000 5 p. c. bonds to run from 15 to 20 yrs.——The St. Louis & San Fran. gen. lien 15-20-yr. 5 p. c. gold bonds (French series) have been listed on the Coulisse of the Paris Bourse. These are the bonds sold to Paris bankers some time ago by Speyer & Co.

Third Ave.—Judge Lacombe, in the U. S. Court, adj. the forecl. sale of the prop. and fran. of the 3d Ave. R. R. Co. until Jan. 11, '10. The adj. was ordered so that the committee of bondholders could prepare a new plan of settlement which could be submit. to the Pub. Serv. Com.

Toledo, St. Louis & Western.—Gross earn. for the yr. end. June 30 were $3,428,-644, as comp. with $3,818,764, and net earn. were $1,202,213, against $1,104,642 in the prev. yr. Oper. exp. were red. being $2,-226,431, against $2,714,032. Other inc. showed a large inc. The surp. remain. after ded. chgs. and taxes was $938,294, which comp. with $417,785.——Co. is earn. at the rate of 7.5 p. c. on the com. stk.

Union Pacific.—The directors elected ex-Judge R. S. Lovett pres. of the co., to succeed the late E. H. Harriman. The other ret. officers were reelectd.——On June 30 U. P. had entirely wiped out its floating debt, incl. bills and loans payable, amtg. last yr. to $41,189,646, and had on hand a work. cap. of $37,401,866, the exc. of quick assets over cur. liab., in add. to $11,083,491 of mat. and supplies, a total exc. of cur. assets of $48,454,357; cash on hand was $26,-990,451, to which is to be added $18,800,000 of demand loans and time dep., or $45,790,-451 of actual money; no part of the 18.87 p. c. shown for its $199,302,300 com. stk. was the result of sale of sec. Oper. of the railroad yielded a surp. after chgs. and pfd. divs. of $19,880,248, or 9.98 p. c. on the com., and inc. from invests., con. of int. and divs. rced. on holdings of sec. of other cos., not of proc. from their sale, amted. to $17,736,-394, or 8.89 p. c. add. on the com. stk., making 18.87 p. c. In add. to the foregoing assets the unpledged sec. of other cos. owned at close of the yr. were $202,947,-525 par val., a dec. on the yr.'s trans. in sale and purch. of sec. of only $2,527,225, par val. Incl. its eq. in $124,200,000 So. Pac.

stk., part of which is pledged, present market val. of avail. stks. and bonds of other cos. in the U. P. treas. on June 30 is approximately $300,000,000.

United Dry Goods Cos.—The com. stk. of the cos. since listing on the N. Y. Stk. Ex. has adv. from 114 to 121½. John Claflin, the pres. of the Asstd. Merch. Cos., as well of the U. Dry Goods Cos., following the recent div. meet., decl. that the biz. amply war. the decl. of 2 p. c. quar. The Asstd. Merch. com. pays quar. 1¼ p. c. reg. and ½ p. c. extra.

U. S. Steel.—Wall St. will be amazed to learn that there is no pool in U. S. St. stks. in which the directors of the co. or its fisc. agts., the house of J. P. Morgan & Co., are in any way int. The U. S. St. Corp. has today over $75,000,000 cash on hand, and had as high as $78,000,000. We can state on auth. of a memb. of the fin. com. of the St. Corp. that from the beginning the corp. has never sold a sh. of St. pfd. or com. except to its employes, and that it has never bought a sh. except for the acct. of its employes. As to there being a stk. mkt. pool in which the directors or J. P. Morgan or J. P. Morgan & Co. are int., we have it on the auth. of three past and present mem. of the house of Morgan & Co. that there is not and never has been any such pool in St. shs. The directors have decl. a quar. div. of 1 p. c. on the com. stk., inc. the an. rate from 3 p. c. to 4 p. c. Three mos. ago the rate was inc. from 2 p. c. to 3 p. c., prior to which ½ p. c. quar. had been main. from Dec. 31, '06. The directors also decl. the reg. quar. div. of 1¼ p. c. on the pfd. stk. The St. Corp. has paid the Hammond Coal Co. $2,000,000 for 27,000 acres of coal lands in the Danville, Ill., dist. In add. the St. people have obt. 10,000 acres from other owners. There has been no pro. falling off in orders for steel. It is est. that the corp.'s shipmts. of steel "for sale" in Oct. were bet. 900,000 and 1,000,000 tons, which is a new high record. It is est. that earns. in Oct. exc. all prev. high rec. for a corres. mo., except Oct., '07, when they were in excess of $17,000,000. If earns. con. as satisf. in Nov. and Dec. as they were in Oct., the surp. for the com. stk. in the fourth quar. will be 4½ p. c.

Utah Copper.—The co. contin. to inc. prod. with steadily dec. costs, the prod. for Sept. amtg. to about 5,363,000 lbs., with a cost of about 7¼ cts. This compl. the 3d quar. of the pres. fisc. yr., and ind. a prod. of 15,300,000 lbs. against 13,774,412 lbs. for the prec. quar., and a prof. of $721,000, against $482,000 for the prec. quar. This is close to $4 a sh. on a 13-ct. metal mkt.

Va.-Caro. Chemical.—Earns. of the co., both gross and net, are breaking all prev. rec. In fact, earns. for the com. are now running at nearly double the '08-'09 fisc. yr. rec., when a bal. of $2,088,593 or 7.1 p. c. was shown for the com. At pres. the co. is earn. better than $13 per sh. on the com.

Wabash.—Gross earns. for first wk. in Oct. were the largest seven days' earns. in the co.'s history, and it is evident that Wab. is getting a goodly sh. of the steel biz. in its ter. The strengthening of the ref. bonds is evidence of the good position of the road. Pfd. and com. stks. have not shared in the reaction of the last fortnight.

Western Maryland.—Pursuant to decree of forecl. and sale made and entered by the U. S. Cir. Court in case of the Equitable Trust Co. of N. Y., trustee, John Hinkley, as special master, will sell at pub. auction on Nov. 19, in Balti., the prop., rights, priv. and fran. of the co.——N. Y. Stk. Exch. has listed the $2,500,000 1st and ref. mtge. 4 p. c. bonds, due '59, recently sold.

Wisconsin Central.—The $2,500,000 first and ref. bonds which have just been listed on the N. Y. Stk. Exch. were handled by the Bk. of Mont. The bonds were distrib. among some four hundred private inv. in London at about 99. They are part of a total issue of $60,000,000 auth. early in Mar. ——A rep. of the Can. Pac. and of the Minn., St. P. & S. Ste. M. says that in all prob. the Wis. Cent. will not begin the paymt. of divs. on the com. stk within the next 12 mos. For the last fisc. yr. the co. failed by $50,000 to earn the div. on the pfd. stk., paymt. of which was begun by the ints. who sold con. of the road thro. the "Soo" Line. In order to pay a div. on the com. stk. during the pres. fisc. yr. it would be neces. not only to make up this def. of $50,000, but to make net earns. largely in exc. of those for the last fisc. period.

Western Union.—By inc. gross earns. $2,000,000 and cutting exp. about the same amt., the co. in the yr. to June 30 was able to show the largest net. rev. in its history. Its oper. ratio was 76, comp. with 88 a yr. ago. The pres. surp. eq. $17,269,277, or abt. 18 p. c. of the total cap. stk.——Co. repts. for last yr. net prof. of $5,614,856, which is 5.6 p. c. on the stk. This comp. with 1.67 p. c. in '07-'08, and an avge. of 6 p. c. for the four prec. yrs.

Westinghouse Air Brake.—About $40,000 was paid out by the co. to salaried empl. in bonuses ranging from $100 to $1,000 each, and more will be disb. in the same manner on succ. pay days. This action on the part of the corp. is cal. to make up for some of the time lost by empl. during the panic of '07. An official said: "The co. desired to show its appre. of the men. The men who stuck to the co. should benefit in the great rush of prosp." It is est. that the co. will pay out several hundred thousand dollars in this manner.

Westinghouse Electric.—N. Y. Stk. Exch. has listed $2,720,000 10-yr. 5 p. c. col. notes, due '17.——Shipments in Sept. approx. $2,250,000; orders agg. $2,500,000. Oct. will show an inc. over Sept. It is understood that the co. in the first six mos. of this yr. earned about 5 p. c. on cap.

INQUIRIES

Is there any point in connection with the science, methods or customs of the various markets which you would like to have elucidated? If so, write questions briefly and they will be answered in this column or otherwise. If personal reply desired, enclose stamped envelope. Address Inquiry Department.

☞ WE DO NOT GIVE ADVICE OR OPINIONS UPON SECURITIES OR PROBABLE MARKET MOVEMENTS.

Less Than Ten Shares on Margin

Will you kindly send me the names of two or three reliable brokers who will buy less than ten shares for me on margin?—L. L. C.

We doubt if any reliable broker will accept orders for less than ten shares on margin. Perhaps, however, if you contemplate putting up about 50 per cent. margin you might find a broker willing to handle the business.

We suggest that you write * * *

Tipsters

Kindly let me have your opinion of the market service called * * *.—H. D. B.

We are not in a position to state from practical experience whether the * * * will make money for you or not, but our opinion of market letters which are widely advertised in flaring type through certain Sunday newspapers, is not such as would lead you to subscribe. If these people could do what they claim, they would not be obliged to sell market letters.

Mining Stocks

J. T.—As you notice from the head of this column, we do not give advice in regard to particular securities. We may say, however, that as a general rule, we think it unsafe to invest in mining companies which are exploited as likely to produce phenomenal profits for purchasers of the stock, unless either you or your friends are able to visit the property and investigate for yourselves. Occasionally such a mine turns out well and yields good profits to the owners of the stock, but these cases are the exceptions. See article on Mining Stocks, Vol. II, p. 78.

Idle Cars

·H. C. K.—The American Railway Association gives its returns in regard to idle cars direct to the newspapers and does not furnish them to private individuals not connected with the railways so far as we are aware. You will find these figures in any good daily paper which has a page devoted to the markets. We are not familiar enough with the Texas papers to refer you to any by name, but we presume any of the larger Dallas or Houston papers would contain this information.

Figuring Price of Bonds

A bond dated 1908 and maturing 1918, drawing interest at the rate of 4½ per cent., is now bid for to net 4.10. How do I figure the amount I should receive for the bond? Do railway companies issue first mortgage bonds convertible into stock?—J. J. F.

A bond dated 1908 and maturing in 1918, 4½ per cent., would sell at about 105½ to net 4.10 per cent. These figures are obtained from a table of bond values. Several such tables are printed. The one we use is Deghuee's, which we can furnish for $3.10 postpaid.

Railway companies sometimes issue first mortgage bonds convertible into stock. There is nothing to prevent their doing this if they desire. This is not a common form of security, however.

Volumes

A. M. M.—Rollo Tape wishes us to say that he doubts if anything can be derived from a study of volumes alone without taking into consideration all the other factors. It all depends on what is happening simultaneously. Whatever can be figured in this connection will appear in the series which is now running in THE TICKER. You will also find some ideas on volumes in back numbers of the magazine.

Discretionary Accounts

J. H. W.—The risks your friends run in connection with the discretionary account mentioned, in addition to the question of personal honesty, are as follows:

The firm with which the operations are carried on may fail, involving a loss of capital. The record which has been made thus far in this discretionary trading is a remarkable one and may not continue. The person who is operating the accounts may become overconfident and take risks that are not warranted. It all depends upon the expertness of the trader, as to how long he can keep up the present pace. If the trading is being done by an incorporated concern, we should look out that the money or dividends are not being paid out of new capital deposited by other people. The history of the Dean Syndicate and of "520 per cent. Miller," as he was called, shows that this is a very likely thing where extraordinary dividends are being maintained.

If you will state the particulars of the present arrangement more fully, sending us some of the concern's literature, we shall be able to form a better opinion as to whether you are now in safe hands.

Financial Literature

What books would you advise every active speculator to purchase in order to be well equipped? Have the following now: "Money and Investments," "The Work of Wall Street," "How Money Is Made in Security Investments," "Crises and Depressions," "A. B. C. of Stock Speculation," "Art of Wall Street Investing," "Pitfalls of Speculation," "Cycles of Speculation," and all numbers of THE TICKER Magazine.—A. S.

You have made an excellent choice of an investment library. We suggest that you now take up the study of intrinsic value of railroad securities. The most useful book for this purpose will be Moody's "Analyses of Railroad Securities." This costs $12.50 postpaid, but it is well worth the money. Notice the announcement of it in the November TICKER advertising pages. We know of no other book that will be of so great help to you in learning how to analyze a corporation and determine the value of its securities.

Bankrupt Stocks

I have been watching the ups and downs of Western Maryland for some time, and at present it seems to be pretty well over its troubles financially. I noticed in one of your numbers that the best time to buy bankrupt railroad stocks is when the last assessment is paid. At present the second preferred certificates are selling at 21, equal to $1 before any assessments were paid. Any advice will be appreciated.—B. B.

You will notice from the heading of the inquiry column in THE TICKER that we do not attempt to give opinions as to the future course of prices or the value of particular securities. The principle laid down, in our article in regard to the best time to buy bankrupt stocks, is unquestionably correct, but such stocks are subject to the general influences of the market just the same as all other stocks. If you pay for your stocks in full you are in no danger of being shaken out on the breaks. If, however, the entire market should have a decline owing to conditions affecting all stocks alike, Western Maryland might easily suffer a temporary decline with the others.

Figuring Averages

Please explain to me the correct method to use in figuring the advance in a stock for several days or a decline in a stock for several days.

Do you consider the Dow-Jones method of figuring averages the correct one to follow for the whole market? They claim that no one stock makes the market, and that you must know what the general list is doing.—J. C. M.

Advances or declines in a single stock are usually figured from closing prices.

The Dow Jones averages also are figured on closing prices. This answers very well as a rough general method of keeping track of the swing of the market. It has its disadvantages, however, as was shown in the panic of May 9, 1901. On that day many stocks declined 50 per cent. of their value, but recovered the greater part of the decline before the end of the session. Please note Mr. Tubb's article in the December TICKER. Also "Studies in Stock Speculation."

To answer your question briefly, either base your averages on closing prices or record for each day the average high price and the average low price, keeping track of both or using the mean price for each day, as you prefer.

We make no charge for answers to inquiries.

Selling Mining Stock Short

You frequently recommend short selling under suitable market conditions. It has occurred to me that a mining boom presents the greatest opportunities in this line. During such periods there are more wildcat propositions placed upon the market than at any other time. The bigger the fake the better the opportunity for short selling. What is your opinion?—W. J. S.

You are right. There are few safer propositions in Wall Street than selling short the class of mining stocks flamboyantly advertised during a mining boom. A number of people make a business of this. When wildcats are offered at $1 a share by the original promotors or "fiscal agents," the short sellers advertise that they will sell it at 90 cents or 80 cents for cash or on the instalment plan, knowing that sooner or later the original "investors" will be glad to sell at any old price they can get. The short sellers cover at such times or when they are forced to deliver the certificate.

One must be careful not to sell a stock that has real merit, as there are sometimes exceptions to the general rule. Once in a while a gold brick stock will pan out and sell at many times its original price. Before the ordinary person can sell one of these stocks short, he must arrange through his broker to borrow the necessary certificate for delivery, and be sure that he can continue to borrow while he remains short. Otherwise he may be forced to go into the market and cover.

Feeling for the Top

I would like to have your opinion on a phase of speculation. Some time ago I shorted St. Paul at 156, covered at 159, sold again at 163⅜, covered at 164⅞, intending to sell again should it reach around 169, but at 165½ it reacted, and not wishing to sell on a declining market, I stopped there. What would have been the proper thing to do at that stage?—J. L.

As a rule, it does not pay to keep feeling for the top of a bull market, as you appear to have been doing, unless you can watch the market closely and have a good knowledge of the technical points involved in stock speculation. The short turns in the market depend almost entirely upon technical conditions, such as the size of the short interest, the position of the long interest—whether in the hands of insiders or margin traders—the amount of commission business being done, the available cash surplus of the banks, etc.

Those who are not in a position to keep well informed on such points as the above usually do better to take an investment position, preferably on the long side, although in some markets the short side is equally safe. Such an investor, however, should not take the short side until a bull market appears to have finally culminated. Then he should endeavor to get short on the rallies during the following decline, and should protect himself with a stop at a distance from the market price varying with the intimacy of his knowledge of the technical situation. It is dangerous business getting in front of a bull market while the steam is still up.

Mechanical Methods

J. L. B.—If a man can show, say one point profit per week, the question of dollars depends upon the amount of capital he is willing to put up and the number of shares he trades in. If he trades in 10 shares, this would pay him $10 a week. If in a hundred shares, he would make $100 a week. In examining the many mechanical methods which have been submitted to us, we pay no attention to the number of shares because so many people are misled by the dollars involved, whereas it is the difference between buying and selling prices which is the sole test of what any method will do.

Mr. Manwaring's method calls for $2,500 capital on each 100 shares, or $250 on 10 shares. If it will produce points it will produce dollars.

We offered to publish anything helpful which you might produce in order to show that we are not in any way prejudiced in favor of Mr. Manwaring. We are after every new idea which develops in connection with the stock market and we expect to print many others, which no doubt our critics will class as advertising, but which we ourselves know that our readers will appreciate. As evidence that the Manwaring articles have helped people, there are some individuals in your own city who have written us that they have been encouraged thereby to work out mechanical methods, which have aided them. This would not have happened had we not printed the above articles.

It was never Mr. Manwaring's intention to state how he does it. Would you do so if you had a money-making idea for which everybody had been searching for years, and which would be destroyed by publicity? Mr. Manwaring cannot be expected to give his method away.

We appreciate your criticisms, and are always glad to hear from you.

Net Earnings—Sympathetic Movements—Reactions—Matched Orders and Wash Sales—Crop Reports—Dow's Theory.

Several of my friends, all of whom, including myself, have not reached the quarter century age limit as yet, desired that I take a "flier" in U. S. Steel, selling it short at 82½. As I had very little knowledge of the stock market, I informed my friends that I did not care to take the "flier" at that time, to which they responded that I had cold feet. They took the "flier" and Steel went up and wiped out 3½ of their 10-point margin. Say, maybe my friends have not cold feet now, together with sore heads!

Instead of taking said "flier," I went up to the free library and looked up U. S. Steel's record. In the latter part of Moody's Manual I saw the advertisement of THE TICKER Magazine, and I immediately sent you my subscription.

Below are several questions that I would like to have elucidated, and if you will kindly give me your good advice, the same will be highly appreciated.

1. I understand that the net earnings of railroads are only published monthly. What publication gives this information at the earliest possible date after the expiration of the month? I want to keep posted on Reading.

2. Will you kindly recommend a legitimate broker in Philadelphia, one suited best for a novice, dealing in, say, 10-share lots?

3. What brokerage house in Philadelphia will furnish Benton's Railroad Quotation Record?

4. When the leaders, such as Reading, U. P. and U. S. Steel, bulge and break, why is it that other stocks act in sympathy?

5. You say, in the October TICKER, that a healthy reaction is from ½ to ¼ of an advance. Does this rule hold good and why? (Accidents are to be excluded in the above.)

6. I do not quite understand "matched orders" and "wash sales," and would like an illustration of their workings.

7. Does the Department of Agriculture issue monthly crop reports? If so, where can I obtain the same?

8. Dow's theory claims that $2,500 will take care of 10 shares on a scale every point down. How can this be done on a stock selling at $75 and declining to $25 per share?

I herewith enclose $1.07 for "Pitfalls of Speculation," by Thos. Gibson. Do you think this to be the best book for me to read next?

I have already read the "Anatomy of a Railroad Report," by Woodlock, Vols. I, II and IV of THE TICKER, "A. B. C. of Stock Speculation" and "The Work of Wall Street," by Pratt.—A. C. S.

It is a pleasure to answer your questions, because you are on the right track and are evidently a close student. We are obliged for your suggestions as to making THE TICKER more interesting to readers. We do not know where you can gain better or clearer information in regard to speculation that from past and current issues of THE TICKER, as it is published for the express purpose of giving such information.

Replying to the questions contained in your letter:

1. The latest net earnings of railroad and industrial stocks are most conveniently obtained from The Investor's Pocket Manual, which we can furnish for 25 cents a month or $2.50 a year. Of course any daily paper having a good financial page will give you net earnings as they come out from day to day. The Philadelphia office of the Reading Co. will tell you by 'phone when earnings are made public, and you can then find them in the daily papers.

2. Few members of the New York Stock Exchange having offices in Philadelphia trade in 10-share lots. We think, however, you will find * * * satisfactory.

3. Any brokerage house with whom you do business should furnish you Benton's Quotation Records on request.

4. When a prominent speculative stock has a severe decline, it is likely to lead those who are long of different stocks on margin to sell out their holdings in other stocks in order to protect themselves on the stock which has the big break. Likewise, on a bulge, shorts may have to protect themselves in a similar way, or bulls who had previously sold out may find themselves again in a position to reinstate their holdings of other stocks. Traders have noticed this fact and have become accustomed to it. They therefore expect other stocks to advance or decline in sympathy with the speculative leaders, and buy or sell such stocks in accordance with their expectations. The result of this is that any prominent advance or decline in a big speculative stock is likely to affect nearly all the other stocks on the list through sympathy. See "Studies in Tape Reading," in Vol. III of THE TICKER, No. 3.

5. When a stock has a pronounced move in either direction, speculators try to go with it, and as a result many of them get long or short, as the case may be. When they start to take their profits this causes a movement in the other direction. Then other traders try to catch on and go with this movement. This is the cause of "healthy reactions," as they are called. There is no absolute rule how far such a reaction will go. In many cases it runs about half the previous movement or a little over half.

6. When a speculator instructs one broker to sell 1,000 Reading at 170 and directs another broker to buy 1,000 Reading at 170, this constitutes a matched order. Of course, it is done for the purpose of making a quotation at 170. A series of such orders may be used to advance or depress prices within a limited range. A wash sale is a nominal sale of stock by one broker to another with the understanding that the transaction is a fictitious one or that such transactions will be balanced off and cancelled at the end of the day. Wash sales are against the rules of the Stock Exchange, and we doubt if such sales take place at the present time. Their importance is historical rather than present. Matched orders cannot be prevented, as the brokers executing those orders do not know that they are matched. They may have suspicions, but cannot be certain. See THE TICKER, Vol. I, No. 5.

7. The Department of Agriculture issues Crop Reports monthly during the growing season. Summaries of these reports are published in all the principal newspapers.

8. Mr. Dow did not claim that $2,500 would enable the trader to purchase 10 shares every point down except under bullish, or at least favorable, conditions. His method was to determine the general trend of the market by averaging 10 or 20 of the principal standard railroad stocks. So long as these averages continued to climb like a pair of stairs, he considered it a bull market and stood ready to begin on a 4 or 5-point reaction and buy stocks every point down on the basis of 10 shares to $2,500 capital. If the movement of the averages later showed that the bull market had turned, he would close out all his long stocks as soon as he could get out even. As he was buying on a scale down and did not begin to buy until after a reaction of 4 or 5 points, he could get out even on a rally of less than half the decline. If you will read this chapter of "A. B. C. of Stock Speculation" more carefully, we think you will have no difficulty in understanding the plan.

We have sent you "Pitfalls of Speculation." We would recommend that you purchase next Henry Hall's "How Money Is Made in Security Investments" and John Moody's "Analyses of Railroad Investments." The latter is the best thing we know to aid you in your study of intrinsic values.

If you wish to be placed in touch with a responsible house, write THE TICKER, stating whether you are contemplating investment or speculation what amount you have for investment, or in what size lots you wish to deal.

Also state what large city is located most conveniently to you, or if you have any preference in this regard.

An Interesting Copper Table

How an Advance in the Price of the Metal Would Affect Different Mines

THE table below was first issued in Hayden, Stone & Company's weekly market letter, then revised and enlarged by Thomas Gibson in his letter of Nov. 6. It presents a very comprehensive view of the copper situation.

One of the points to be noticed is that an advance in the price of copper metal will benefit the high cost producers, such as Amalgamated, Anaconda, Butte, or Tennessee, more *in proportion* than it will benefit the newer low cost producers, such as Utah or Nevada Consolidated.

Table Showing Comparative Position of Leading Copper Companies

	No. of Shares.	Present Annual Rate of Production.	Cost per Lb.	Earnings per Share 13c. Copper.	Per Cent. on Market Price.	Earnings per Share 14c. Copper.	Per Cent. on Market Price.	Earnings per Share 15c. Copper.	Per Cent. on Market Price.	Price Nov. 1, 1909.
Amalgamated	1,538,879	220,000,000	9½	$5.00	5.82	$6.43	7.49	$7.86	9.16	85⅞
Anaconda	1,200,000	90,000,000	10	2.25	4.66	3.00	6.22	3.75	7.77	48¼
Butte Coalition	1,000,000	35,000,000	10	1.05	3.70	1.40	4.93	1.75	6.17	28⅝
Calumet & Arizona	200,000	28,000,000	9	5.60	5.60	7.00	7.00	8.40	8.40	100
Calumet & Hecla	100,000	85,000,000	8½	36.25	5.41	44.75	6.68	53.24	7.95	670
Copper Range	384,188	33,500,000	9½	3.05	3.77	3.92	4.85	4.79	5.92	80⅝
Granby	135,000	25,000,000	10	5.56	5.70	7.40	7.59	9.25	9.49	97½
Greene-Cananea	2,500,000	45,000,000	10½	0.45	3.87	0.63	5.42	0.81	6.97	11⅝
Mohawk	100,000	12,000,000	10½	3.00	5.00	4.20	7.00	5.40	9.00	60
Nevada Consol.	1,600,000	60,000,000	7	2.25	8.96	2.62	10.43	3.00	11.94	25⅛
North Butte	400,000	45,000,000	9	4.50	7.63	5.62	9.53	6.75	11.44	59
Old Dominion	300,000	33,000,000	10½	2.75	5.24	3.85	7.33	4.95	9.43	52½
Osceola	100,000	29,000,000	10¼	7.97	5.08	10.87	6.92	13.77	8.76	157
Quincy	110,000	21,500,000	10⅝	4.89	5.56	6.84	7.77	8.79	9.99	88
Shannon	300,000	18,000,000	11½	0.90	5.67	1.50	9.45	2.10	13.23	15⅞
Superior & Pittsburg	1,500,000	25,000,000	9½	0.58	3.46	0.75	4.48	0.92	5.49	16¾
Tennessee	200,000	15,000,000	10½	1.87	5.19	2.62	7.28	3.37	9.36	36
Utah Consol.	300,000	15,000,000	9	2.00	4.57	2.50	5.71	3.00	6.86	43¾
Utah Copper	735,000	60,000,000	8	4.08	8.24	4.90	9.90	5.72	11.56	49½
Wolverine	60,000	10,000,000	7½	9.17	6.11	10.83	7.22	12.50	8.33	150
Average, 20 cos.	638,153	45,250,000	9.54	5.16	5.46	6.58	7.16	8.00	8.86	93.80

Finance Forum Opens

Interesting Course of Wednesday Night Lectures Laid Out at West Side Y. M. C. A.

The scope of the courses in finance offered by the Y. M. C. A. in New York has been greatly widened as compared with last year. The array of financial experts who will deliver lectures this year is indeed remarkable. Over sixty lecturers are included, among whom are such well known authorities as the following:

Horace White, Chairman Hughes' Investigating Committee.

Henry Clews, author "Fifty Years in Wall Street."

Charles A. Conant, author "Money and Banking," "Modern Banks of Issue," etc.

Elbert H. Gary, Chairman Board of Directors, United States Steel Corporation.

Thomas Gibson, author "Pitfalls of Speculation," "Cycles of Speculation," etc.

Henry Hall, author "How Money Is Made in Security Investments," etc.

Edwin R. A. Seligman, Professor Political Economy, Columbia University.

Thomas F. Woodlock, author "Anatomy of a Railroad Report," etc.

Roger W. Babson, author "Standard Business Barometers."

George B. Cortelyou, formerly Secretary of the Treasury of the United States.

Theodore E. Burton, author "Financial Crises and Commercial Depressions."

John Moody, author "Art of Wall Street Investing," "Analyses of Railroad Investments," etc.

Montgomery Rollins, author "Money and Investments," "Bond Values," etc.

Sereno S. Pratt, Secretary New York Chamber of Commerce; author "The Work of Wall Street."

The Bond Buyer's Guide

Showing Comparative Yield of Principal Railroad Issues Listed on the New York Stock Exchange

IN the following table we have arranged in order the principal active issues of bonds listed on the New York Stock Exchange, income being figured at the latest available selling price. Ratings are according to classifications given in Moody's "Analyses of Railroad Investment." It will be noted that convertible bonds, of any class, give a relatively lower yield than others.

These tables appear each month, and are invaluable to bond buyers, as well as to brokers and all others who are called upon to recommend or advise on such matters.

Class Aaa—Bonds of the highest grade as regards security and which are also readily convertible into cash. These issues are not likely to be affected by any normal changes in the earning power of their respective roads; their prices are, however, influenced by the rates for money.

Description.	Due.	Interest period.	Price Nov. 9, '09.	Yield.
Chicago, Mil. & St. Paul Mineral Point Div. 1st 5s	1910	J — J	100⅛	4.88
Southern Pacific C. P. stock. col. 4s.	1949	J — D	90¼	4.53
Oregon Short Line Guar. ref. Col. 4s.	1929	J — D	93½	4.50
Nor. Pacific & Gt. Nor. C. B. & Q. Col. Joint 4s	1921	J — J	95⅞	4.45
Texas & Pacific 1st 5s	2000	J — D	113	4.41
Lake Shore & Mich. So. Deb. 4s	1928	M — S	94¾	4.41
Lake Shore Deb. (25 years) 4s	1931	M — N	94½	4.39
Pennsylvania Conv. 3½s.	1915	J — D	95¾	4.35
Hocking Valley Con. 4½s	1999	J — J	103½	4.36
Central Pacific 30 Yrs. Col. 3½s	1929	J — D	88¾	4.36
Toledo & Ohio Cen. 1st 5s	1935	J — J	110½	4.32
Chicago & Alton ref. G 3s	1949	A — O	75	4.32
Wabash 1st G. 5s.	1939	M — N	112	4.28
Rio Grande Western Tr. 1st 4s.	1939	J — J	95½	4.27
Denver & Rio Grande 1st Con. G 4s.	1936	J — J	96½	4.22
Northern Pacific Ry. Gen. Lien 3s	2047	Qu. F	72	4.19
Chicago, Mil. & St. Paul Chicago & Lake Sup. 5s	1921	J — J	108½	4.14
Central Pac. Ref. 1st 4s.	1949	F — A	97¼	4.14
Union Pacific 1st Lien Ref. 4s	2008	M — S	97⅞	4.10
Louisville & Nashville Unified G. 4s.	1940	J — J	98½	4.09
Oregon Ry. & Navigation Con. 4s	1946	J — D	98½	4.08
Nor. & Western Ry. Con. 1st 4s.	1996	A — O	98⅝	4.06
Chicago, R. I. & Pacific Gen. 4s	1988	J — J	99¾	4.05
Illinois Central 1st Ref. 4s	1955	M — N	99	4.05
Chicago, Bur. & Quincy. Neb. Ext. 4s	1927	M — N	99⅝	4.03
N. Y., Chicago & St. Louis 1st 4s	1937	A — O	99½	4.03
Reading Co. Gen. G. 4s.	1997	J — J	99⅞	4.03
Chicago, Bur. & Quincy, Ill. Div., 3½s.	1949	J — J	89⅝	4.03
Atch., Top. & S. F. Gen. Con. 4s	1995	A — O	100⅛	4.00
Atchison, Top. & S. F. Gen. G. 4s.	1995	A — O	99⅞	4.00
Chicago, Mil. & St. Paul Series B Gen. 3½s	1989	J — J	88	4.00
Illinois Central L. N. O. & T. Col. Tr. G 4s	1953	M — N	100½	3.98
Chicago, Bur. & Q. Ill. Div. 1st 4s	1949	J — J	100⅝	3.97
Central of New Jersey Gen. 5s	1987	J — J	125⅝	3.94
Chicago & Northwestern Gen. 3½s	1987	M — N	89¾	3.93
Northern Pacific Prior Lien 4s.	1997	Qu. J	102¼	3.91
West Shore 1st 4s.	2361	J — J	103¾	3.88
Chicago, Mil. & St. Paul Series A Gen. 4s	1989	J — J	103½	3.86
N. Y. Central & H. R. ref. 3½s.	1997	J — J	91	3.86
Union Pacific Id. gr. G. 4s.	1947	J — J	103	3.85
Lake Shore 1st 3½s.	1997	J — D	91¾	3.83
Illinois Central 1st 4s	1951	J — J	104⅝	3.79
Pennsylvania Con. G 4s	1948	M — N	104½	3.78
Delaware & Hudson Conv. Deb. 4s	1916	J — D	101⅞	3.70
Chicago, Mil. & St. Paul Gen. G 4s	1919	J — J	103	3.67
Chicago, Bur. & Q. Deb. 4s	1913	M — N	101⅝	3.56
Pennsylvania R.R. Conv. 3½s	1912	M — N	99⅞	3.54
Albany & Susquehanna 1st Con. 3½s	1946	A — O	101½	3.43

Class Aa—Composed of bonds but slightly inferior to the above, either as to security or salability or both.

Wabash 2nd G. 5s.	1939	F — A	101	4.94
Canada Southern 1st 6s	1913	J — J	104½	4.75
Colorado & Southern Ref. & Ex. 4½s.	1935	M — N	97¾	4.65
Michigan Central 20 Year Deb. 4s	1929	A — O	92⅜	4.59
Central of Georgia Con. G 5s	1945	M — N	109¼	4.48
Kansas City Southern 1st G. 3s.	1950	A — O	73¾	4.39
N. Y. Central & H. R. R.R. Lake Shore Col. 3½s	1998	F — A	80⅝	4.37
N. Y. Central Deb. 4s.	1934	M — N	94½	4.36
East Tenn., Va. & Georgia Con. 1st 5s	1956	M — N	113½	4.33
Atchison, Top. & S. F. Short Line 4s.	1958	J — J	94	4.29
Southern Pacific R. R. 1st ref. 4s.	1955	J — J	94⅝	4.27
Atlantic Coast Con. 1st G. 4s.	1952	M — S	95¾	4.22
Chesapeake & Ohio 1st Con. 5s	1939	M — N	113¼	4.21
Colorado & Southern 1st G. 4s.	1929	F — A	97⅜	4.20
Rome, Watertown & Ogdensburg 1st Con. 5s	1922	A — O	109	4.10
Reading Cen. of N. J. Col. G 4s	1951	A — O	98	4.10
Cleveland, Chicago, Cin. & St. Louis Gen. G 100 Yr. 4s	1993	J — D	98	4.08
Baltimore & Ohio Prior Lien 1st G 3½s	1927	J — J	93	4.05
Baltimore & Ohio 1st G. 4s.	1948	A — O	99¼	4.04
Minn., St. Paul & S. S. M. Con. 4s.	1938	J — J	99¼	4.04
Chicago, Bur. & Quincy Gen. Mtg. 4s.	1958	M — S	99¼	4.03
Missouri, Kansas & Texas 1st G. 4s.	1990	J — D	99½	4.02
Nor. & Western Conv. 10-25-yr. 4s.	1932	J — D	100½	4.00
Norfolk & Western Div. 1st Lien and Gen. 4s	1944	J — J	93	3.39
Atchison, Top. & S. F. Conv. 4s.	1955	J — D	120⅛	3.17
Union Pacific 20-yr. Conv. 4s.	1927	J — J	114⅜	2.96
Atchison, Top. & S. F. 10-yr. Conv. G. 5s.	1917	J — D	120¼	2.23

Class A—Bonds of high grade, but liable to be affected by changing earning power as well as by money rates.

Kansas City, Ft. Scott & M. Ref. Con. G 4s	1936	A — O	82	5.26
Chicago & Alton 1st Lien 3½s	1950	J — J	74	4.99
Missouri Pacific Lexington Div. Col. 1st 5s	1920	F — A	101½	4.81
Erie 1st Con. G. Prior Lien 4s.	1996	J — J	84	4.78
Missouri Pacific Col. Trust G. 5s.	1917	M — S	101⅝	4.76
Chicago & Eastern Illinois Ref. & Imp. 4s	1955	J — J	86⅛	4.75
Chicago, R. I. & Pacific 1st Ref. G. 4s.	1934	A — O	90½	4.64
Missouri Pacific 1st Con. 6s	1920	M — N	112	4.60
Missouri, Kansas & Texas 2nd G. 4s.	1990	F — A	87¾	4.58
Colorado & So. Ft. W. & Den. C. 1st G 6s	1921	J — D	113½	4.53
Atlantic Coast Line L. & N. Col. 4s	1952	M — N	90⅛	4.52
Louisville & Nashville South-Monon Joint 4s.	1952	J — J	91	4.47
Baltimore & Ohio P. L. E. & W. Va. Ref. 4s	1941	M — N	93	4.41
Baltimore & Ohio So. West. Div. 1st G 3½s	1925	J — J	89⅞	4.39
Chesapeake & Ohio Gen. G. 4½s.	1992	M — S	102¾	4.38
St. Louis Southwestern 1st G 4s Bd. Ctfs.	1989	M — N	91⅞	4.37
St. Louis, Iron Mt. & So. Gen. Con. & Land Gr. 5s	1931	A — O	109¼	4.34
St. Louis & San Francisco Mo. & W. Div. Gen. G 6s	1931	J — J	109¼	4.34
Louisville & Nashville, Atl. Knox & Cin. Div. 4s.	1955	M — N	94	4.30
Long Island R.R. Con. Unified 4s	1949	M — S	96¼	4.19
Southern Pacific 20 Year Conv. 4s	1929	M — S	102¼	3.84

Class Baa—Good second grade bonds, slightly speculative.

Erie Con. & Gen. Lien G 4s	1996	J — J	75¾	5.30
Toledo, St. L. & Western 1st 4s	1950	A — O	81	5.11
St. Louis & I. Mt. Unified and Ref. G 4s	1929	J — J	87	5.04
Ann Arbor 1st G. 4s.	1995	Qu. J	81	4.96
St. Louis, I. Mt. & So., R. & G. Div. 1st 4s.	1933	M — N	87¼	4.91
Missouri, Kansas & Texas 1st Ref. 4s	2004	M — S	85¼	4.67
Cincinnati, Dayton & Ironton 1st 5s	1941	M — N	108	4.52
Wisconsin Central, Sup. & Dul. Div. & Term 1st 4s.	1936	M — N	93	4.45
Wisconsin Central, 50-yr. 1st Gen. 4s.	1949	J — J	94⅞	4.27
N. Y., N. H. & Hartford Non-conv. Deb. 4s	1956	M — N	95⅞	4.21
N. Y., N. H. & Hartford Conv. Deb. 6s.	1948	J — J	134⅞	4.18
N. Y., N. H. & Hartford Conv. 3½s. Deb.	1956	J — J	98½	3.57

Class Ba—Well secured bonds, but likely to decline if earnings fall off or advance if earnings increase.

St. Louis & San Fran. 15-20 Year Gen. Lien 5s	1927	M — N	89¾	5.92
Erie Conv. 4s Series B	1953	A — O	71⅝	5.77
Wabash 1st Ref. & Ext. G. 4s.	1956	J — J	73⅞	5.60
Denver & Rio Grande, 1st & Ref., 5s.	1955	F — A	94	5.36
Missouri, Kansas & Texas Gen. S. F. 4½s.	1936	J — J	90¼	5.17
Erie Conv. 4s Series A	1953	A — O	80½	5.12
Fort Worth & Rio Grande 1st 4s	1928	J — J	88	4.99
Iowa Central 1st G 5s	1938	J — D	105¼	4.68
Southern Ry. 1st Con. G. 5s.	1994	J — J	108⅜	4.61

Class B—Issues likely to fluctuate in price and more speculative than the foregoing class.

St. Louis Southwestern 1st Con. G. 4s.	1932	J — D	77½	5.67
Iowa Central Ref. G. 4s.	1951	M — S	76	5.46
Chicago, R. I. & Pac. Col. tr. 4s.	2002	M — N	76⅞	5.22
Missouri Pacific 40-yr. Col. G. Loan 4s.	1945	M — S	80⅞	5.17
St. Louis & San Francisco Ref. G. 4s.	1951	J — J	84	4.90
Southern Ry. Mob. & Ohio Col. Tr. S. F. 4s	1938	M — S	89⅞	4.64

Class Caa—Almost directly responsive to changes in earning power, and having an average available income less than double interest requirements.

Southern Ry. Dev. & Gen. G Series A 4s	1956	A — O	80⅝	5.09

The Market Outlook

Summary of the Situation and Opinions of the Best Authorities

TO put it in two words, prices of securities have now advanced to the level where the rising interest rate is beginning to act as a buffer and impede their further advance. Inexperienced investors are apt to resent this rise in the interest rate as a sort of unnecessary interference with otherwise prosperous business conditions. But are prices to go on rising forever? There must be something to set the limit, and the amount of money available for the transaction of business is as good a limit as any. The gradual rise of the rate of interest acts as an automatic and slightly yielding check on active speculation just as the governor checks the runaway engine.

Foreign Money Rates.—European money rates are now about at the point which was reached in the second or third year preceding each of the panics of 1884, 1893, 1903, and 1907. This does not necessarily mean that our next panic will come in 1912, as many other factors enter into the situation. It does, however, serve roughly to establish our present place in the cycle of price movements.

Domestic Money Rates.—Requirements for crop moving and for business have drawn money from New York to the interior, thus lessening the supply of funds for use in the stock market. The bulk of this movement is generally over by the end of the first week in December. In 1908 the return flow began about December 1. It is likely to be somewhat later this year, as the prosperity of the farmers leads them not only to retain more money for use, but also to hold their crops for higher prices, thus making the crop movement later.

A deficit in New York bank reserves has so far been avoided by the automatic shifting of loans from clearing-house banks to private banking houses or to individual investors, as a result of higher interest rates thus obtainable. No serious deficit will be shown this year. Any temporary deficit will be quickly restored.

An unfavorable feature is the considerable excess of loans over deposits shown by the three largest New York banks—National City, National Bank of Commerce, and First National.

General Business.—Bank clearings and railway earnings continue to increase, and the outlook is for unprecedented business activity in practically all lines during 1910.

Commodity Prices, as shown by Bradstreet's index number, have advanced 56.7 per cent. since 1896, and 10.5 per cent. since November, 1908. They are now close to the highest record ever reached. This means prosperity for producers, but paring down expenses by those having fixed incomes; a good outlook for stocks which get the benefit of these prices in dividends, but a poor prospect for bonds, from which investments are likely to be diverted by better opportunities elsewhere.

New Financing.—For the above reason, new issues of securities are likely to be of stocks rather than of bonds. Four leading roads are already issuing $200,000,000 new stock, and other large issues are pending. The sale of such new stock will naturally lessen the demand for existing securities, and probably marks the beginning of the third, or distributive stage of the grand cycle of prices.

Politics and Labor.—President Taft is doing just what he said he would do—endeavor to carry out Roosevelt's policies—yet many "conservative" financiers seem grieved. Anti-railroad sentiment was merely checked by the panic. The railways have sown the wind by everywhere antagonizing the small shipper through discrimination, delays, discourtesy and outright damage. Further railroad legislation is certain and must be reckoned upon.

It is figured that, in the last 12 years, commodity prices have advanced 45 per cent. and the average wages of railway employees only 20 per cent. As a result, employees are demanding a raise. As wages and salaries represent 41 per cent. of railway gross earnings, this is an important consideration.

Summary of Opinions of Recognized Authorities. — High-priced rails appear to have seen the top for the present. Low priced rails should advance early in 1910. The good industrials are headed for still higher prices, in anticipation of boom times. The movement of all prices will be irregular, with frequent ups and downs. An active shake-out is possible between now and January 1, but if it comes stocks will be a purchase. Bonds may rally with easy money next spring, but will continue dull.

November 20, 1909.

Contents of Volume V.

THE TICKER, November, 1909, to April, 1910.

SUPPLY AND DEMAND LETTER

W. D. GANN SCIENTIFIC SERVICE INC.
78 WALL STREET, NEW YORK

1929 ANNUAL STOCK FORECAST

Projected Curve #1 and Main Trend which the 30 Industrial Stocks
should follow:-

ojected Curve #2 which Industrial Stocks in strong position should
ow:-

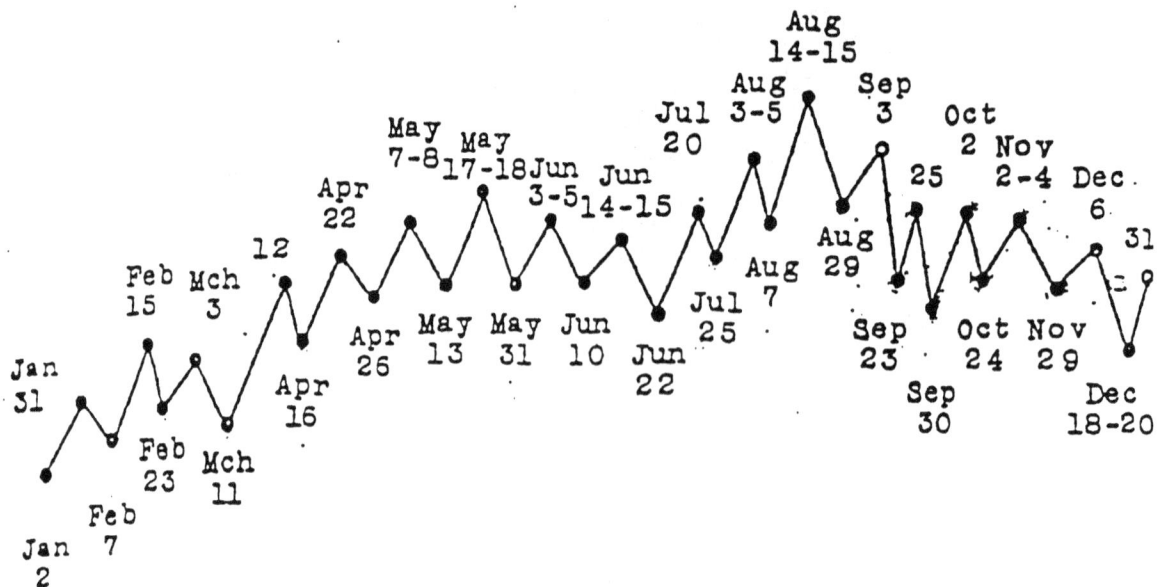

Jan
31

Feb
15

Mch
3

12

Apr
22

May
7-8

May
17-18

Jun
3-5

Jun
14-15

Jul
20

Aug
3-5

Aug
14-15

Sep
3

Oct
2

Nov
2-4

Dec
6

31

Apr
26

May
13

May
31

Jun
10

Jun
22

Jul
25

Aug
7

Aug
29

25

Sep
23

Oct
24

Nov
29

Jan
31

Feb
23

Mch
11

Apr
16

Jan
2

Feb
7

Sep
30

Sep
18-20

ojected Curve which Railroad Stocks should follow:-

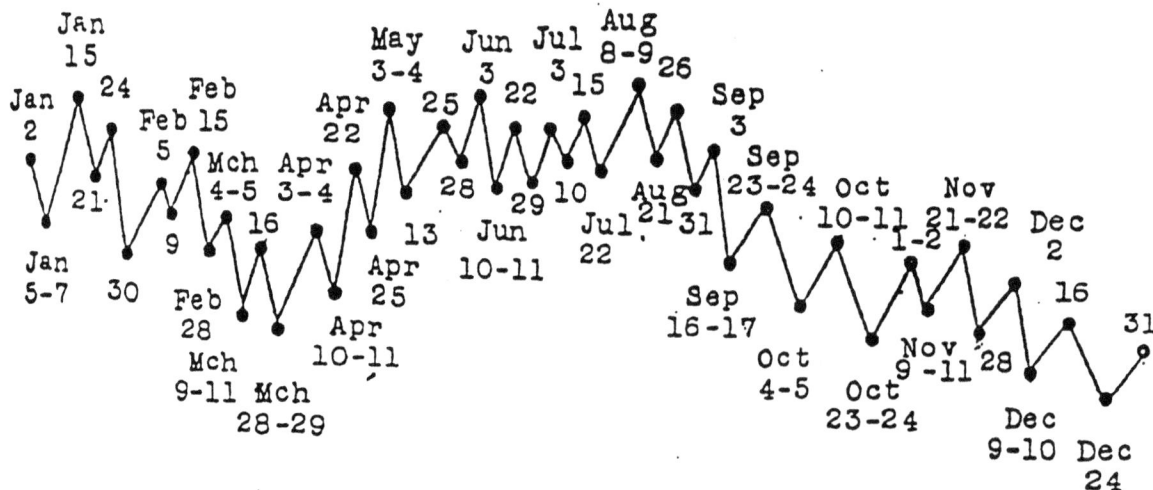

Jan
15

Jan
2

24

Feb
Feb 15

5

May
3-4

Apr
22

25

Jun
3

22

Jul
3
15

Aug
8-9

26

Sep
3

Sep
23-24

Oct
10-11

Nov
21-22

Dec
2

Jan
5-7

30

9

Mch
4-5

Apr
3-4

16

13

28

29

10

Jul
22

Aug
21
31

Aug

Oct
1-2

16

31

21

Feb
28

Apr
25

Jun
10-11

Sep
16-17

Nov
9-11

28

Mch
9-11

Apr
10-11

Oct
4-5

Oct
23-24

Dec
9-10

Dec
24

Mch
28-29

GENERAL OUTLOOK FOR 1929

This year occurs in a cycle which shows the ending of the bull
:et and the beginning of a prolonged bear campaign. The present
. campaign has lasted longer than any previous campaign in the
.ory of this country. The fact that it has run longer and prices

have advanced to such abnormal heights means that when the decline sets in, it must be in proportion to the advance. The year 1929 will witness some sharp, severe panicky declines in many high-priced stocks.

The history of the stock market has always been that it discounts prosperity and that in doing so prices always advance too far. In other words, the stock market runs too far ahead of prosperity and the first decline is only a readjustment back to what stocks should sell according to their merit and investment return. Then, when business depression sets in and earnings start to show falling off, stock prices continue to go lower, discounting unfavorable business conditions.

But such groups of stocks as the oils, sugars, rubbers and some of the agricultural stocks, which have been depressed and declined while other stocks advanced, will record much higher prices in 1929. New and popular industries will continue to prosper, such as, radio, airplane, chemical and electrical concerns. This is the electrical age. People take quickly to new inventions, especially those which provide for the convenience and comfort of living. This will increase the earnings of concerns manufacturing new electrical appliances.

Many stocks will be distributed and will work lower while the stocks in strong position work higher. With such a varied list of stocks representing so many industries in different parts of the country, it is not reasonable to suppose that they would follow the same trend by an means.

More and more business is getting into the lines of mass production, mergers and consolidation. The big companies are getting the business while the smaller companies find it harder to get business enough to return a fair amount on their capital stock.

During the early part of the year, business conditions will not be up to general hopes and expectations. In the Spring and Summer business will improve and the outlook generally will be cheerful. But again in the Fall of the year depression will set in and unfavorable business conditions will cause big declines in stocks. Money rates will be high the greater part of the year.

During the year 1928 the public have entered the stock market on the largest scale ever known in history. Foreigners have bought our stocks more than at any time since or prior to the outbreak of the World War. The American public is no longer making safe investments in stocks. They have the gambling fever and are buying everything regardless of price, simply buying on hope that stocks will continue to go up. This is a dangerous situation and has always resulted in a big decline. There will be no exception in this case.

The man who makes money buying stocks in 1929 will have to use greater discrimination than ever before in selecting the right stocks to buy. When once stocks have reached final top and start on the way down, they will continue to work lower and rallies will get smaller. Those who hold on and hope will have big losses. The markets will move over a very wide range and sharp, severe declines will be followed by quick rallies. It will be necessary most of the time for a trader to be very nimble and change position quickly in order to take advantage of the opportunities as they develop in an active market.

WHAT WILL CAUSE THE NEXT DEPRESSION IN BUSINESS AND DECLINE IN STOCKS?

PROSPERITY! The great wave of prosperity which this country has experienced during the past few years has been in many ways responsible to the stock market. The great increase in the value of stocks has increased the borrowing power of various companies and has permitted expansion and even inflation. The pendulum has swung so far in one direction that many people have forgotten that it can ever swing back in the other direction, but one extreme always follows another and it will not fail at this time. Stocks, like water, always seek their level.

The great earnings of many large corporations during the past year can not be expected to continue. Over-confidence is just as bad as extreme pessimism. It is just as easy for a big man to make a mistake as it is a little man. In my judgment many of the wisest speculators who have made large fortunes out of this bull campaign will overstay their market and be caught just the same as they have in the past. Then when the decline gets under way and they try to liquidate in a bear market, they will bring about a real smash in prices. It is one thing to mark stocks up to dizzy heights and quite another thing to be able to sell all of them near top prices. As stocks decline, forced selling both by pools and the public always comes into the market and causes prices to go lower than they naturally would if there had not been over-speculation. The public never has been considered good leaders in a bull market. The fact that they are now in the market in greater numbers than ever before makes the technical position of the market more dangerous.

INFLATION:- The volume of trading on the New York Stock Exchange during 1928 was the largest in history and at this writing the total sales for the year have exceeded 750,000,000 shares and will approach 900,000,000 by the end of the year. Stock Exchange seats have had the greatest advance in history. Brokers' loans doubled in 1927 and 1928. Such enormous volume of trading at extreme high levels with feverish markets and wide fluctuations can mean only one thing, - that the pools and insiders have taken advantage of public buying to liquidate stocks and when once they have sold all they have to sell, they will not support the market. With the public so heavily involved in such large numbers and being unable to support the market, when once the decline gets under way, it will be more sharp and severe than ever before. Loans will be called and bankers will make new loans only on the very best security. We will hear of many stocks being thrown out of loans.

Another contributing factor to inflation was our large holding of gold but this has changed materially during 1927 and 1928
when more than half a billion of gold has flowed out to foreign
countries and there are no prospects that it will not continue
during the next few years.

INSTALMENT BUYING:- People are still living beyond their
means and instalment buying continues on a large scale. We believe
it will yet prove to be the greatest menace to business and to the
prosperity of the country. When depression sets in and unemploy-
ment increases and people are unable to pay for goods which they
have bought on a credit, buying power will be reduced and many
companies will not only lose business but will lose money on goods
sold on a credit.

AGRICULTURAL SITUATION:- Has been so unfavorable during the
past few years that the Government has had to devise means to help
the farmer and no doubt President Hoover will see that some law is
passed to remedy this condition. However, we are in a cycle which
is likely to produce crop failures or a series of small crops for
some years to come. This will reduce the purchasing power of the
farmer and help to bring about deflation in stocks.

PROSPERITY COMPLEX:- The recent wave of seeming prosperity
has been due to the psychological effect on people. They have
watched stocks go wild in the past three years until they are
hypnotized into believing that every concern and everybody is
prosperous, but facts do not confirm it. During 1927 about 45% of
all concerns making income tax returns showed a loss in business
and 1928 will not be much better. It is now a survival of the
fittest. The small businesses are failing more every year. Conditions are changing so fast that many old firms are being forced out
of business. Electricity and oil are taking the place of coal and
wood. Automobiles supplanted the horse, and the railroads, despite
the large increase in population and business, have not shown as
great earnings as they did 20 years ago. Many industries have not
been prosperous for some time. The textile, coal and agricultural
industries have suffered. The oil situation has been bad until
recently. The rubber industry has been demoralized by low prices.
Sugar has been at low levels for the past two years. When people
realize that prosperity is not general and confined to only a few
lines, then they will have the "panic complex."

PUBLIC CONFIDENCE:- As long as the public believes that
everything is all right, they will hold on and hope, but when public buying power has exhausted itself and the largest number of
stock gamblers in history lose confidence and all start to sell,
it requires no stretch of imagination to picture what will happen.
When the time cycle is up, neither Republican, Democrat, nor our
good President Hoover can stem the tide. It is a natural law.
Action equals reaction in the opposite direction. We see it in the
ebb and flow of the tide and we know that from the full bloom of

summer follows the dead leaves of winter. Gamblers do not think; they always gamble on hope and that is why they lose. Investors and traders must pause and think, look and listen, and get out of stocks before the great deluge comes.

WAR.:- Our great prosperity has caused jealousy throughout the world, and as conditions get worse in foreign countries, greed and jealousy will lead to war. It is the hungry dog that starts the fight. A study of the rise and fall of nations shows that when any country enjoys unusual prosperity for a long period of time, war is one of the main causes of the start of depression. While we hear a lot of talk about peace, the facts show that many of the leading foreign countries as well as our own country, are spending more money preparing for war than ever before in their history. When a man or a country is armed and gets ready to fight, he usually gets what he is ready for.

FOREIGN COMPETITION:- Germany is rapidly coming back and competition for trade will be keener in the coming year. Many of the other foreign countries are making desperate efforts to regain their pre-war trade and will make progress along these lines, which will hurt our business.

INDUSTRIAL STOCKS

MAIN TREND OR MAJOR SWINGS

The Industrial Curve this year is based on the Dow Jones' 30 Industrial Stock Averages. Previously the Dow Jones' Averages, which are published by the Wall Street Journal, were based on 20 industrial stocks, but in the latter part of 1928, they changed from 20 to 30 and our Curve is based on the 30 Industrial Stocks. The stocks now used in these Averages are:- Allied Chemical, Am. Can, Am. Smelting, Am, Sugar, Am. Tobacco B, Atlantic Refining, Bethlehem Steel, Chrysler, Gen. Electric, Gen. Motors, Gen. Ry. Signal, Goodrich, Int. Harvester, Int. Nickel, Nash Motors, Mack Trucks, North American, Paramount, Postum, Radio, Sears Roebuck, Stand. Oil of N. J., Texas Corp. Texas Gulf, Union Carbide, U. S. Steel, Victor Tk., Westinghouse, Woolworth, Wright Aero.

From the low level in August, 1921, to the high level in November, 1928, the 20 Industrial Stocks recorded an advance of about 230 points, the greatest advance in history. The fact that these Averages advanced nearly 100 points during 1928 is unparalleled in history. This year is like 1906, 1916, and 1919, when such violent fluctuations were witnessed and large volume of trading took place, only to be followed the year after by a panicky decline.

The minimum between extreme high and extreme low during 1929 for the 30 Industrial stocks will not be less than 50 points and the maximum fluctuation may be as much as 90 to 100 points. This means that many of the high-priced stocks will fluctuate 150 to 200 points between extreme high and extreme low prices. The lower-

priced stocks will move in a narrower range and will not make as
much as the minimum between extreme high and low.

Most of the Dow Jones' 30 Industrial Stocks will follow
Curve #1 very closely. The high point for most of these stocks
will be reached around January 12th. After that time prices
should gradually work lower and the trend should be down until
around March 28th to 29th, when bottom will be reached for
another bull campaign. Many stocks will reach bottom around
March 14th to 15th and remain in a narrow trading range until the
bull campaign starts in April. When the advance gets under way,
some stocks will reach top for the year in May, others in June
and some of the others which are behind the market will reach
final high in August as shown by Curve #1 and Curve #2. A large
majority of stocks will not go any higher than the highs reached
in the month of July. After July and early August, the main trend
will be down and some sharp declines will take place, prices working lower and reaching first bottom around September 27th to 28th.
From this level follows a fair-sized rally and a trading market
running into the early part of November. After that, the big bear
campaign will get under way and stocks continue to work lower,
reaching extreme low level for the year around December 23rd to
24th.

There are now over 1500 stocks listed on the New York Stock
Exchange and often in one day over 800 different issues are
traded in. Therefore, the 30 Industrials and 20 Rails do not
always represent the main trend or curve of the market and many
stocks will run in opposition to this trend. That is why I am
giving you Curve #1 and Curve #2 on Industrial stocks.

Industrial Curve #2 represents the stocks which are in
strong position and many of which are not included in the Dow
Jones' 30 Industrials. Many of these stocks have declined during
1928 and have been accumulating. They will advance while other
stocks decline. Curve #2 indicates low around January 2nd followed by an advance up to January 31st; a decline to February 7th
and high of next rally around February 15th. Then prices will
work lower, making bottom around March 11th. Watch the stocks
that make bottom at this time as they will be the ones to lead the
advance. After the low in March, this Curve continues to work
higher with only moderate reactions until high is reached around
May 17th to 18th. From this top a bigger decline will take place.
The last low is indicated around June 22nd. From this level the
stocks which are in strong position and behind the market will
gradually work higher, some of them reaching top during July
while others will not reach final top until August 14th to 15th.
After this top is reached heavy liquidation will start and prices
will work lower from every rally. First decline culminates
around September 30th; then a rally making top on October 2nd,
followed by a decline to October 24th; then a final top around
November 2nd to 4th, followed by a big decline, reaching bottom
around December 18th to 20th; then a rally to the end of the year.

Below is a list of stocks in strong position which should follow closely Industrial Curve #2. They will be the best stocks to buy on reactions:-

Ajax Rubber	Cont. Baking A	Loft	Sinclair Oil
Amerada	Cont. Motors	Lee Rubber	So. Porto Rico Sug.
Am. Agri. Ch.	Cuban Am. Sug.	Lehn & Fink	Spicer Mfg.
Am. Beet Sug.	Curtiss Aero.	Louisiana Oil	S. O. of Calif.
Am. Bosch Mag.	Davison Chem.	Mack Trucks	S. O. of N. J.
Am. Brake Sh.	Dome Mines	Magma	S. O. of N. Y.
Am. Drug	Elec. Pr & Lt.	Mallinson	Sun Oil
Am. & For. Pr.	Elec. Storage	Maracaibo	Superior Oil
Am. Ship & Com.	Fisk Rubber	Marland	Tennessee Cop.
Am. Steel Fdy.	Foundation	Mex. Seab.	Texas Corp.
Am. Sugar	Glidden	Mid-Cont. P.	Texas Pac. C. & O.
Am. Woolen	Goodrich	Nat. Pr & Lt.	Texas Gulf Sul.
Anaconda	Goodyear	Nevada Cons.	Transcont. Oil
Armour A	Granby	N.Y.Airbrake	U. S. Rubber
Assd. Dry Gds.	Gt. Nor. Ore	Otis Steel	U. S. Smelt.
Austin Nichols	Gt. West. Sug.	Packard	Va. Car. Chem.
Barnsdall A	Hupp	Panhandle	Ward Baking B
Beechnut	Indian Ref.	Pan Pete B	Warner Pictures
Bethlehem St.	Inspiration	Park Utah	Westinghouse Elec.
Booth F.	Int. Comb. Eng.	Pathe Ex A	White Eagle
Briggs	Int. Mar. Pfd.	Phillips P.	White Motors
Cal. & Hecla	Jones Tea	Pillsbury Fl.	Willys Overland
Central Alloy	Kelsey Hayes	Reo Motors	Wilson & Co.
Cerro de Pasco	Kelvinator	Republic Iron	Worth Pump
Chandler Clev.	Kennecott	Reynolds Spg.	Wright Aero
Chile Copper	Kresge S. S.	Royal Dutch	Yellow Truck
Congoleum	Lago Oil	Shell Union	Producers & Ref.
Cons. Textile	Loews	Simms Pete	

The stocks given in the list below are the ones which have been distributed and are the best to sell short around the dates indicated for top on Curve #1. These stocks will have the greatest declines, especially in the early part of the year and again from August to December when a big bear campaign is indicated.

Allis Chalmers	Chrysler	Int. Harvester	Timken
Allied Chemical	Coca Cola	Kroger	Tobacco Products
American Can	Cont. Can	Mathieson Al.	Union Carbide
Am. Intern'l	Corn Products	Mont. Ward	U. S. Ind. Alcohol
Am. Linseed	Dupont	Reynolds "B"	U. S. Steel
Am. Locomotive	Gen. Electric	Sears Roebuck	Vanadium
Am. Radiator	Gen. Motors	Shattuck F. G.	Victor Talking
Am. Smelting	Hudson Motors	Stewart Warner	Woolworth
A. M. Byers	Houston Oil	Studebaker	

RAILROAD STOCKS

MAIN TREND OR MAJOR SWINGS

The Railroad Curve is based on the Dow Jones' 20 Railroad Stock Averages published by the Wall Street Journal. The issues used in these Averages are as follows:- Atchison, Atlantic Coast, B. & O, Canadian Pacific, Ches. & Ohio, Rock Island, Del. Lackawanna & Western, Erie, Illinois Central, Louisville & Nashville, N. Y. Central, New Haven, Norfolk & Western, Northern Pacific, Pennsylvania, Pere Marquette, Southern Pacific, Southern Railway, Texas & Pacific, and Union Pacific.

From the low in June, 1921, to the high in November, 1928, these Railroad Averages advanced nearly 80 points. They have made the highest price in history, getting above the extreme high level recorded in 1906. The fact that they advanced into new territory in the latter part of 1928 shows the possibility of many rails which are in strong position going higher during 1929. But the fact that during prosperous times the railroads have been unable to earn an average of 6% on their capitalization does not make them very attractive from a speculative standpoint. Only those which have merit and show large earnings will have very big advances during 1929.

The fluctuations between extreme high and extreme low during 1929 are not likely to be less than 20 points and the average may be as high as 30 to 35 points, which means that many high-priced stocks will fluctuate 50 to 75 points between extreme high and low.

The Rails as a rule follow the forecast trend better than the Industrials because they represent only one group of stocks while the Industrials represent fifteen or twenty different groups. The Dow Jones' 20 Railroad Stock Averages are representative of the railroad group and most of the railroads will follow Curve #1 very closely, therefore it is not necessary to give Curve #2 this year.

Railroad Curve #1, you will notice on Page #2, runs down from January 2nd and bottom is indicated around the 5th to 7th. Top for the month of January is indicated around the 15th and after this date the main trend is down, prices working lower and reaching first bottom around March 9th to 11th and second bottom around March 28th to 29th. Accumulation should take place around this time and a bull campaign should start. First top is indicated around May 3rd to 4th; then a decline, followed by an advance with second top, possibly a little higher, around June 3rd. Then another decline and irregular market, reaching low level around June 28th and 29th. After that prices will work higher until around July 15th; then decline to the 22nd, followed by an advance to around August 8th to 9th, when final top on rails should be made for another big decline. After this top, prices will work lower from every rally. A big decline is indicated for September; another sharp decline in October, reaching bottom around the 23rd to 24th; then a rally running to around November 21st to 22nd followed by a decline to December 24th, when the 20 Rails will reach the lowest price of the year.

The following Rails are in the strongest position and should

have the greatest advances at the times when the bull campaigns
are indicated:-

Atlantic Coast Line	Del. Lackawanna & W.	Missouri Pacific
Bangor & Aroostook	Erie	New Haven
Brooklyn Man. Transit	Gt. Northern Pfd.	Northern Pacific
Chicago Gt. Western	Hudson & Manhattan	Seaboard Air Line
C. M. & St. Paul Com.	Kansas City Southern	Wabash Common
C. M. & St. Paul Pfd.	Mo. Kansas & Texas	Western Maryland

The Railroad stocks given below are those which are in the
weakest technical position; have had advances and show distribution. They will be the best short sales on rallies during the
times that the Forecast indicates declines.

Atchison	Lehigh Valley	Pittsburgh & W. Va.
Baltimore & Ohio	Louisville & Nash.	Reading
Canadian Pacific	N. Y. Central	St. Louis & San Fran.
Chesapeake & Ohio	Norfolk & Western	St. Louis & S. W.
Rock Island	Pere Marquette	Southern Pacific
Delaware & Hudson	Texas & Pacific	Southern Railway
	Union Pacific	

POSITION OF THE VARIOUS GROUPS

With the large number of stocks now listed on the New York
Stock Exchange representing the various industries throughout this
country and foreign countries, and as these different groups of
stocks are affected by supply and demand and the varying conditions
in the different parts of the United States and by events which
transpire in foreign countries, it is impossible for them to all
reach extreme high or extreme low on the same date or even in the
same year or the same month. The different time element of the
various stocks and groups of stocks will cause some to advance
while others decline. Therefore it is well to watch the individual
stocks. Watch those that make top in May, those that make top in
June and those that make top in August. The ones that make top in
the early part of the year and fail to reach higher levels in July
or August, will be the ones to lead the decline, because they will
have had longer time for distribution. Guard against selling
short the late movers until they have had time to complete distribution. You will receive a list of stocks in strongest position
and those in weakest position with the Supplement on the first of
each month.

The Dow Jones' 30 Industrial stocks are representative of
the active industrials and most of them will follow the Industrial
Curve very closely, but some of the individual stocks which are
in strong or weak position will vary from this Curve and make tops
and bottoms at different times. These special stocks and their
position will be covered in the Supplements each month.

The New York Herald Tribune Averages on 70 stocks are a
more active and reliable trend guide now than the Dow Jones' 30

Industrials. I am giving the stocks used in these Averages because I will often refer to them in the Supplements issued on the first of each month during the year. The range of these 70 stocks between extreme high and low should not be less than 40 points and will probably reach as high as 70 to 80 points. They take in the representative stocks from the following groups:-

COPPERS:- Am. Smelting, Anaconda, Cerro de Pasco, Calumet & Ariz.,
    Greene Cananea, Kennecott and Tennessee Copper & Chemical.
EQUIPMENTS:- Am. Car & Fdy., Baldwin Loco, Gen. Ry Signal, Pullman.
FOODS:- Am. Sugar Pfd., Armour & Co. of Del. Pfd., California
    Packing, Corn Products, Nat. Biscuit.
MANUFACTURING:- Allied Chemical, Allis Chalmers, Am. Can, Am.
    Radiator, Am. Tobacco, Burroughs Add. Machine, Chicago
    Pneumatic Tool, Coca Cola, Columbian Carbon, Eastman Kodak,
    Endicott Johnson, General Electric, Int. Bus. Machine, Int.
    Harvester and U. S. Rubber.
MOTORS:- General Motors, Chrysler Motors, Chrysler Motors Pfd.,
    Jordan, Hudson, Mack Truck, Stewart Warner, Stromberg,
    Studebaker, White.
OILS:- Atlantic Refining, California Petroleum, Houston, Marland
    Oil, Pan American Pete "A", Pure Oil Pfd., Standard Oil of
    Calif., Standard Oil of N. J., Texas Company and Union Oil
    of Calif.
STEELS:- Bethlehem, Crucible, Gulf States, Sloss Sheffield,
    U. S. Steel, Vanadium.
STORES:- Gimbel Bros., Macy, Montgomery Ward, Sears Roebuck and
    Woolworth.
UTILITIES:- American Express, Am. Tel. & Tel., B'klyn Edison,
    Columbia Gas, Cons. Gas, Detroit Edison, Peoples Gas,
    Western Union.

    A review of the above groups showing those in the strongest and weakest position will be sent with the Forecast or given in the Supplements each month.

IMPORTANT DATES FOR CHANGE IN THE MAJOR TREND

    The following dates should be watched for important changes in the major trend of both Industrial and Railroad stocks. If any stock makes top or bottom around any of these dates, you can expect a reversal in trend, especially if there is a sharp decline or a sharp advance around these dates:- Feb. 8th to 10th, March 21st to 23rd, May 3rd to 7th, June 20th to 24th, August 3rd to 8th, Sept. 21st to 24th, Nov. 8th to 11th, Dec. 20th to 24th. These dates are based upon a permanent cycle which does not change. Important tops and bottoms are made in many stocks every year around these times. Watch the stocks that reach extreme high or low levels around these dates.

DATES FOR ACTIVITY AND WIDE FLUCTUATIONS

    The following dates indicate times when stocks will be very

active and have wide fluctuations, making tops and bottoms. While all stocks will not make tops and bottoms around these dates, some of the most active ones will and if you watch the ones that turn around these dates, it will prove helpful in your trading:-

January 5th to 7th, 12th to 15th, 18th to 24th.

February 9th to 12th, 20th to 22nd, and 27th to 28th.

March 10th to 11th, very important for change in trend; 21st to 22nd important; 28th to 29th another very important date for change.

April 3rd, 9th to 10th, 13th to 15th, 21st to 23rd.

May 3rd to 4th- watch stocks that make top around this date; 9th to 11th another important date when some stocks will make bottom and other stocks will make top. 22nd to 23rd and 29th to 31st- very important dates for change in trend; watch for stocks that will make top around this date.

June 1st to 2nd- quite important; 7th to 10th another important change; 21st to 23rd a more important change.

July 3rd to 5th- very important for change in trend; 9th to 10th also quite important; 21st to 24th more important.

August-- One of the most important months for change in trend. Many stocks will start on their long down trend. 7th to 8th- quite important; 16th to 17th important; 23rd to 24th important; 29th to 30th of minor importance.

September 2nd to 3rd important; 16th to 17th important; should be bottom of a panicky decline. 21st to 24th important for top; 27th and 28th important for bottom of a big break.

October 2nd; 8th to 9th; 16th to 20th very important, - watch stocks which start to decline and go with them; 26th to 28th minor importance.

November 10th to 22nd- a very important period for wide fluctuations. Airplanes, radio and some electrical stocks may have sharp advances. Other important dates for changes are 1st to 2nd, 17th to 19th, and 24th to 25th.

December 1st to 2nd important; 16th to 17th of minor importance; 23rd to 24th greater activity and of major importance.

The above dates are not only important for changes in trend and times when bottoms and tops should be reached, but on these dates important news is indicated and some will be of a sudden, unexpected nature, at times favorable and at other times unfavorable, but causing stocks to be active and fluctuate, making tops and bottoms and changing trend.

HOW TO TRADE WITH THE FORECAST

The time given for tops and bottoms is the most important factor for you to know and watch. It makes no difference about the price a stock is selling at. So long as you KNOW WHEN it will reach low or high levels you can buy or sell and make money. When the Forecast indicates bottom at a certain date and stocks decline, you should buy the ones given as in strong position or the ones we recommend buying and place a stop loss order 3 to 5 points away according to the price the stock is selling at. With stocks that

sell at $200 to $300 per share, it is often necessary to use a
stop loss order 10 points away because you have an opportunity to
make large profits and can afford to take a greater risk.

Watch the action of stocks around the dates when the Forecast shows that tops or bottoms are indicated and when they hesitate for a few days and fail to make new high or low levels, you
should get out and reverse position. Keep up charts and follow
the rules in my book, Truth of the Stock Tape, and you will be able
to follow the Forecast to better advantage and make more profit.

Do not expect the Averages or individual stocks to advance
or decline as many points as shown on the graph or Projected Trend.
This is only a guide to show you when big swings and activity are
indicated. For example:- Industrial Curve #1 begins at "0" on
January 2nd and runs down to "7" on January 5th to 7th, a decline
of 7 points on Averages. Some high-priced stocks may decline 10
to 20 points at this time while other low and medium-priced stocks
will decline only 2 to 5 points. While some stocks which are late
movers and in very strong position will follow Curve #2 and move
up during January at the same time that high-priced leaders decline, the main thing is that Curve #1 shows a sharp advance from
January 5th to 7th up to January 12th and Curve #2 shows up trend
all the month of January. Therefore you should watch for a decline and buy the strong stocks around January 5th to 7th; then
watch for top January 12th to 15th, sell out and go short of the
stocks which are in our short sale list. Then on January 30th,
if there has been a big decline as shown by Curve #2, you should
cover shorts and buy for a rally and if stocks advance to February
13th to 15th, watch for top, sell out longs and go short because
Curve #1 indicates a big decline the last half of February and during March.

The big buying opportunity will come in March. Around March
10th to 11th and 28th to 29th, you should buy the best stocks to
hold for the Spring bull campaign into late May. Both Curve #1
and #2 indicate a big decline from July and August to December,
therefore from July and August you should play the short side and
wait for rallies to sell short rather than buy on breaks because
the main trend will be down and you should never buck the trend
but go with it.

Remember you must buy and sell at the right time regardless
of prices. No matter how high stocks are, if they are going higher, you should buy. It makes no difference how low they are; if
the trend is down and they are going lower, you must sell short
and go with the trend. Take a loss quickly if you see that the
Forecast is off or you have picked the wrong stock. Do not hold
on and hope. Delays are dangerous. It is easy to make back
small losses, but hard to regain big ones. Follow the rule, -
cut short your losses and let your profits run. Learn to act
quickly. How much better to take action now than to trust to un-
certain time. You can always get in the market again so long as
you have money. New opportunities always come if you have patience
and cash to take advantage of them.

1929 PREVIEW

JANUARY, FEBRUARY AND MARCH

While the new year opens under favorable conditions and you will hear much about great prosperity and the newspapers will be optimistic for the future, the bright outlook is likely to be clouded with war or complications in foreign countries. Trouble is threatened to the United States thru Mexico or Japan. Peace pacts are likely to be broken. Spain and France will arouse opposition. Agitation over religion in some of the foreign countries will disturb peaceful conditions.

Great storms are indicated in the south and southwestern parts of the United States during the early Spring. Much loss and damage by fire. In March when President Hoover takes office, if some law has not already been passed, he will advocate having one passed to help the farmers. This will cause an advance in commodities and in turn help agricultural stocks. Airplane concerns will make rapid progress in the Spring and from a panicky depressed stock market in February and March, a Spring bull campaign will take place. Steel business will be quite active. Electrical concerns will do a large business and there will be a boom in oil stocks.

APRIL, MAY AND JUNE

The Spring Quarter indicates unfavorable weather for starting crops. Storms and rains and danger of a tidal wave along the Gulf of Mexico. Commodity prices will advance and business in general will improve. A wild wave of speculation in oils, coppers, rubbers, sugars and airplane stocks will make this a very active period. Along in May or June foreign competition will begin to hurt business in some lines in this country. This will cause a depressing effect on stocks and they will decline.

JULY, AUGUST AND SEPTEMBER

During this period some of the foreign countries will prosper and we will have great competition to face. War or trouble with foreign countries is threatened. A very mixed market during this period with some stocks advancing while others decline. Speculation will shift from stocks to commodities on account of short crops. Foreign crops will be short in some of the countries. Storms and unseasonable weather will cause damage.

August will be marked by many electric storms and damage by fire. Some new discoveries will help chemical stocks around this time. Germany and France will make great strides in aviation.

September:- A great change in business conditions will set in around this time which will cause a severe decline in the stock market. Textile and woolen stocks will prosper and these will be among the last stocks to advance. During the months of April, August, September, and October, there is danger of war and trouble thru foreign countries.

OCTOBER, NOVEMBER AND DECEMBER

Settlement of the debt question with France will again come to the front. Other countries will arrange some favorable agreement in regard to trade which will cause business depression here. A great change in the business outlook will set in as we near the end of the year. Corporation earnings will show depreciation and be disappointing.

The month of October indicates some advance in mining stocks. The oil and sugar stocks will be among the last to advance around this time. During November the chemicals and oils will have a boom for a short time and make final top. In December foreign business with South American countries will be good, but we will have competition from some of the European countries.

MONTHLY INDICATIONS

J A N U A R Y

The new year starts off under favorable conditions, but profit-taking will start and stocks will sell off sharply the first few days. Then good buying will appear and an advance will start. The oils, rubbers, chemicals, and airplanes will lead the advance, reaching top around the 12th to 15th. Around the 18th to 24th some rails, electrics and steels will advance. Some trouble in foreign countries, probably Germany or France, will have an unfavorable effect and will help to start the decline here. Watch for top; sell out long stocks and go short. Quite a decline will take place to the end of the month.

INDUSTRIAL STOCKS indicate extreme high for the month around the 12th to 15th; extreme lows around the 5th to 7th and 30th. Minor moves:- January 2nd decline should start; 5th to 7th bottom of decline. Heavy buying should start around this time and a sharp advance should take place, making top around the 12th. 19th bottom of decline; 24th top of rally; then follows heavy selling and a sharp decline, reaching bottom around the 30th.

RAILROAD STOCKS indicate extreme high for the month around the 15th; extreme low around the 5th to 7th and 30th. Minor moves: January 2nd top, when decline should start; 5th to 7th bottom for quite a rally; 15th top of strong rally, when another decline should start; 21st bottom of decline; 24th top of rally. From this top a big decline should take place reaching low for the month around the 30th.

Dates to watch for change in trend:- The dates marked "XX" are the most important and indicate a major change in trend. You should watch for important changes around these dates. The dates marked "X" only indicate minor changes in trend which will only last for a few days. -- January 5th-7th XX, 11th-12th X, 25th-26th XX, 31st X.

F E B R U A R Y

Business will fall off and we will hear some discouraging reports. The Federal Reserve Bank will make some change or threaten to curb speculation. There will be talk of new banking laws, which may be adverse to speculation. The general list of high-priced stocks will decline this month, altho the market will be mixed. Sugars, rubbers and late movers will have some advances. The railroad, airplane, radio, and electric stocks will rally from every decline. Around the 12th to 13th of the month some of the oils, rubbers and sugars will be quite strong. The general list of old time leaders, however, will work lower from every little rally.

INDUSTRIAL STOCKS indicate extreme high for the month around the 13th to 14th and extreme low around the 28th. Minor moves:- 1st to 4th advance; then follows a decline to the 8th, when bottom should be reached for another quick rally; 13th to 14th top, sell out and go short. Expect heavy liquidation and a sharp, severe decline reaching bottom around the 28th for a moderate rally.

RAILROAD STOCKS indicate extreme high for the month around the 15th and extreme low around the 28th. Minor moves:- 1st to 5th advance and make top for a moderate decline; 9th bottom of decline; expect quick rally in some rails, reaching high around the 15th, followed by a sharp decline making bottom around the 28th.

Dates to watch for change in trend:- 9th to 12th XX; 19th to 20th XX; 23rd to 24th X, 28th X.

M A R C H

Mr. Hoover will take the office of President of the United States this month and in the early part of the month there will be a demonstration in stocks and quite an advance, but it will not hold and a sharp, severe decline will take place in many stocks before the end of the month. Some trouble is likely to come up in connection with Spain or Mexico which will upset the market. Airplane stocks will be quite strong during the dates indicated for advances to take place. The oils, sugars and chemicals will hold up better than other stocks. Traction stocks will be strong and there is likely to be some development in connection with the subway fare which will cause an advance in New York traction stocks. The steels, motors, rails, and electrical issues will break during the early and latter part of the month.

INDUSTRIAL STOCKS indicate extreme high for the month around the 4th to 5th; extreme low around the 28th to 29th, altho some stocks will reach low for the month around the 14th to 15th. Minor moves:- 1st to 5th strong advance. The market will be discounting President Hoover's inauguration. A sharp decline follows, making first bottom around the 14th to 15th; then a quick rally in many stocks reaching top around the 20th, followed by heavy liquidation and a sharp decline to around the 28th or 29th when final bottom will be reached for another bull campaign. This is the time to buy the stocks in strong position as they will have sharp advances and work higher into the summer.

RAILROAD STOCKS indicate extreme high for the month around the 4th to 5th; extreme low around the 9th to 11th and 28th-29th. Minor moves:- 1st to 5th strong market. Stocks behind the market will lead the advance. From the top around the 4th to 5th quite a sharp decline will take place, culminating around the 9th to 11th; then follows a moderate rally reaching top around the 16th; then another decline, making final bottom around the 28th to 29th when you should buy the stocks in strong position for an advance which will last into the early days of May.

Dates to watch for change in trend:- 4th to 5th X; 10th to 11th XX; 16th X; 21st to 23rd X; 28th to 29th XX.

A P R I L

The public will again come into the market on a large scale and there will be a wild wave of speculation, especially in the oils, coppers, rubbers, sugars and airplane stocks. The chemicals, airplanes and radio stocks will have rapid advances. Some action by the Government or law passed will cause a break which will run down to around the 15th. Money rates will be quite high. 16th to 30th- General news will be more favorable and stocks will have better advances. Foreign trade will increase, especially with the South American countries.

INDUSTRIAL STOCKS indicate extreme low for the month around the 12th to 13th and extreme high around the 20th to 22nd. Minor moves:- 1st to 3rd top of quick advance; 12th to 13th bottom for another big advance; 20th to 22nd top of sharp rally; then follows a decline making bottom around the 26th to 27th when stocks should be bought for another advance, running to the end of the month and continuing into May.

RAILROAD STOCKS indicate extreme low for the month around the 10th to 11th and extreme high around the 20th to 22nd, altho they will be quite strong and some will make higher just at the end of the month. Minor moves:- 1st to 3rd-4th quick advance; then follows a moderate decline, reaching bottom around the 10th to 11th, when a sharp advance will take place, stocks running up fast and making top around the 20th to 22nd, followed by a reaction to the 25th; then a strong advance to the end of the month.

Dates to watch for change in trend:- 2nd to 3rd X; 9th to 10th X; 13th to 15th XX; 21st to 23rd XX; 26th to 27th X.

M A Y

This is a month for great activity in the stock market. We will hear some very bullish news about general business conditions. There will be some large combines, consummation of mergers; large financial deals will take place and there will be much talk of continued prosperity, all of which will cause the public to buy stocks at the top. General news will be very bullish and stocks will fluctuate over wide ranges. Some stocks will reach high around the early part of the month and have a break around the middle of the month. There will be a boom in rubbers, sugars, oils, airplane, radio and electrical stocks. These will be the leaders. Watch for top and sell out. Do not overstay your market as a big break will take place in June.

INDUSTRIAL STOCKS indicate extreme high for the month around the 29th to 31st and extreme low around the 9th to 10th. Minor moves:- 1st to 4th quick rally, making top for a sharp reaction; 9th to 10th bottom of decline; buy for another sharp advance; 16th top of rally, but only for a minor reaction; 20th-bottom of reaction. Stocks in strong position will have a rapid advance between the 10th and 29th. Watch for top around this time.

RAILROAD STOCKS indicate extreme high for the month around the 3rd to 4th; extreme low around the 11th to 13th, altho some issues will go to extreme high around the end of the month. Minor moves:- 1st to 3rd strong market, making top around 3rd to 4th. Then follows a decline, making bottom around the 11th to 13th, followed by an advance making first top around the 25th for a moderate reaction to the 28th; then rally to the end of month.

Dates to watch for change in trend:- 3rd to 4th X; 9th to 10th XX; 22nd to 23rd X; 29th to 31st XX.

J U N E

A sharp decline and heavy liquidation in many stocks is indicated for this month. There will be war in foreign countries or war rumors. Strikes at home as well as abroad. Crop news will be unfavorable. Storms or earthquakes on the southern border and in Mexico will do damage and help to unsettle the market. The outlook for the summer business will be very much mixed. One of the major cycles and time factors runs out this month and a very important change in trend is indicated. High-priced stocks will have rapid declines and many stocks will make extreme high for the year. The tin, oils and agricultural stocks and also the chemicals will break badly after reaching top in the early part of the month. Motors will also decline sharply.

INDUSTRIAL STOCKS indicate extreme high for the month around June 1st; extreme low around the 22nd to 24th. Minor moves:- 1st to 2nd advance and make top for a big decline; 10th to 11th bottom of sharp decline; then follows a moderate rally reaching top around the 17th, followed by heavy liquidation and sharp decline making bottom 22nd to 24th. From the 24th to the end of the month many stocks will have quite a rally.

RAILROAD STOCKS indicate extreme high for the month around the 3rd; extreme low around the 10th to 11th and 28th to 29th.

The rails will not move in a very wide range this month, except a few of the very high-priced issues. Minor moves:- 1st to 3rd advance; 4th to 10th-11th sharp decline; then follows a moderate rally, reaching top around the 21st to 22nd followed by liquidation and lower prices, making bottom for the month 28th to 29th.

Dates to watch for change in trend:- June 1st to 2nd XX; 7th to 10th X; 21st to 23rd XX; 28th X.

J U L Y

Another advance will take place this month and many stocks will have sharp rallies and reach the final high for the year. The airplane companies will prosper and their stocks will advance. Electrical and chemical stocks will also record sharp advances. Pools will rush up stocks as fast as they can to unload. The late movers will be brought into line while distribution is taking place in the old time leaders. Sugars and rubbers should have some sharp advances. A very important major time factor ends at this time and indicates the starting of a big prolonged bear campaign. Remember that the last high for the year will occur in many stocks. A great deluge and panicky decline will follow the top at this time, resulting in a "Black Friday" in September. There are likely to be some labor troubles and strikes in the west and south which will interfere with the business outlook.

INDUSTRIAL STOCKS indicate extreme high for the month around the 20th; extreme low around the 9th to 10th. Minor moves: 1st to 3rd strong market, making top for a quick decline; 9th to 10th bottom of sharp decline; then follows a rapid advance, making top on the 20th; decline, reaching bottom on the 22nd; followed by a strong market to the end of the month.

RAILROAD STOCKS:- The rails will move in a comparatively narrow range this month. Extreme low is indicated around the 9th to 10th and 22nd; extreme high around the 15th. Minor moves:- 1st to 3rd advance; then follows a decline making bottom around the 9th to 10th; a quick rally to the 15th; then follows a sharp decline reaching bottom on the 22nd, followed by an advance to the end of July.

Dates to watch for change in trend:- 3rd to 5th XX; 10th X; 21st to 24th XX; 30th to 31st X.

A U G U S T

A few of the late movers will advance this month and reach final high. Chemical stocks will be among the last to advance. The steels and oils will be strong for awhile and the sugars and rubbers will make final top. Unfavorable news will develop which will start sharp declines and the long bull campaign will come to a sudden end. Money rates will be high and final top will be reached for a big bear campaign. Stand from under! Don't get caught in the great deluge! Remember it is too late to sell when everyone is trying to sell. There will be electric storms which will cause damage to crops and heavy losses are indicated thru fires.

INDUSTRIAL STOCKS indicate extreme high for the month around the 7th to 8th; extreme low 29th to 30th. Minor moves:- The first of the month starts in strong and prices run up fast reaching top around the 7th to 8th; then heavy selling will take place and a sharp decline will follow, bottom being reached around the 16th to 17th, but only for a small rally; 23rd to 24th top of rally, followed by heavy liquidation and lower prices, making bottom for the month around the 29th to 30th.

RAILROAD STOCKS indicate extreme high for the month around the 8th to 9th, althosome industrial stocks and rails among the late movers will hold up and not make top until the 14th to 15th as indicated on Curve #2. Extreme low for the month for rails indicated around the 30th to 31st. Minor moves:- 1st- advance will start and prices will run up fast, making top around the 8th to 9th; then follows a fast decline, reaching bottom around the 20th to 21st followed by moderate rally to around the 25th; then a sharp decline making low for the month on the 30th to 31st.

Dates to watch for change in trend:- 7th to 8th XX; 16th to 17th X; 23rd to 24th XX; 29th to 30th XX.

S E P T E M B E R

One of the sharpest declines of the year is indicated. There will be loss of confidence by investors and the public will try to get out after it is too late. Storms will damage crops and the general business outlook will become cloudy. War news will upset the market and unfavorable developments in foreign countries. A "Black Friday" is indicated and a panicky decline in stocks with only small rallies. The short side will prove the most profitable. You should sell short and pyramid on the way down

INDUSTRIAL STOCKS indicate extreme high for the month around the 2nd to 3rd; extreme low 27th to 28th. Minor moves:- 2nd to 3rd top of moderate rally. Heavy liquidation will break out around this time. Unfavorable news will develop and a sharp, severe decline will take place, reaching first bottom around the 16th to 17th, but only for a small rally. 20th to 21st top of moderate rally followed by another heavy wave of liquidation, carrying prices down to extreme low levels around the 27th to 28th, from which level a moderate rally will follow.

RAILROAD STOCKS indicate extreme high for the month around the 3rd; extreme low at the end of the month. Minor moves:- 1st to 3rd advance. Liquidation will start around this time and a sharp decline will follow, carrying prices down to around the 16th-17th; then a moderate rally on short covering with top around the 23rd-24th, followed by a sharp decline running down to the end of the month.

Dates to watch for change in trend:- September 2nd to 3rd XX 16th to 17th XX; 21st to 24th X; 27th to 28th XX.

O C T O B E R

General business conditions will be getting worse and the country will suffer from the over-speculation. Money rates will be high and bankers will call loans, causing some sharp declines in stocks after rallies. The chemical, electrical and airplane stocks will hold up and have some quick rallies around the dates indicated for advances.

INDUSTRIAL STOCKS indicate extreme high around the 18th to 19th; extreme low around the 8th to 9th and 26th to 28th. Minor moves:- October 2nd top of small rally from which a sharp decline will take place; 8th to 9th bottom of decline, when a better advance will take place, especially in the stocks in strong position; 18th to 19th top of rally. Stocks in weak position will have a sharp decline, running down to the 26th to 28th; then follows a moderate rally to the end of the month.

RAILROAD STOCKS indicate extreme high for the month around the 10th to 11th; extreme low 23rd-24th. Minor moves:- 1st to 4th decline and make bottom for a moderate rally; 10th to 11th top of rally; then follows a heavy wave of liquidation and lower prices making bottom around the 23rd to 24th, followed by a moderate advance to the end of the month.

Dates to watch for change in trend:- 2nd to 4th XX; 8th to 9th X; 18th to 20th XX; 26th to 28th X.

N O V E M B E R

The oils, chemicals and rubbers will have a final advance this month and make top for another decline. Business conditions will be growing more unfavorable. There are likely to be earthquakes in Mexico or California. This will disturb the stock market and depress business. This is the month for war news from foreign countries and some great leader abroad will show his power. The latter part of the month is very unfavorable and some sharp declines will take place. But the airplane, radio and electrical companies and some of the rails will have an advance around the 10th to 22nd.

INDUSTRIAL STOCKS indicate extreme high for the month around the 2nd to 4th; extreme low around the 23rd to 25th. Minor moves:- 1st to 4th advance and make top for a sharp, severe decline; then follows heavy selling and a sharp decline, reaching bottom around the 11th to 12th, but only for a moderate rally; 18th to 19th top of advance. From this level there will be another sharp, severe decline carrying prices down to low levels around the 23rd to 25th. Then follows a moderate rally to the end of the month.

RAILROAD STOCKS indicate extreme high for the month around the 21st to 22nd; extreme low around the 27th to 28th. Minor moves:- 1st to 2nd top of moderate rally; then follows a decline, reaching bottom around the 9th to 11th; then a quick rally, making top around the 21st to 22nd followed by heavy liquidation and a sharp decline, making bottom around the 27th to 28th.

Dates to watch for change in trend:- 1st to 2nd XX; 11th to 13th X; 17th to 19th XX; 24th to 26th X.

D E C E M B E R

Our business in some of the foreign countries will increase. Speculation will shift from stocks to commodities. The U. S. Government is threatened with great opposition, if not danger of war. General business outlook will grow very much more unfavorable Panicky declines in stocks will take place.

INDUSTRIAL STOCKS indicate extreme high for the month around the 2nd; extreme low around the 23rd to 24th. Minor moves:- 1st to 2nd advance; then follows a sharp, severe decline and heavy liquidation with only small rallies indicated lasting one to two days, reaching extreme low around the 23rd to 24th; then follows a quick rally reaching top on the 28th followed by decline to the 31st.

RAILROAD STOCKS indicate extreme high for the month around the 2nd; extreme low around the 24th. Minor moves:- 1st to 2nd advance; 3rd to 10th sharp decline, making bottom for only a moderate rally; 15th top of rally; then heavy liquidation and a decline running to the 24th; then follows a rally to the end of the month.

Dates to watch for change in trend:- 1st to 2nd XX; 16th to 17th X; 23rd to 24th XX; 28th X.

This Forecast is PRIVATE AND CONFIDENTIAL and for your personal use only. For your own protection do not permit others to copy or use it.

November 23rd, 1928.

Recommended Readings

Learn before you lose AND forecasting by time cycles, W. D. Gann, www.therichestmaninbabylon.org

New Stock Trend Detector: A Review of the 1929-1932 Panic and the 1932-1935 Bull Market : With New Rules for Detecting Trend of Stocks, W. D. Gann, www.therichestmaninbabylon.org

How to Make Profits In Commodities, W. D. Gann, www.therichestmaninbabylon.org

45 Years in Wall Street, W. D. Gann, www.therichestmaninbabylon.org

The Magic Word, W. D. Gann, www.bnpublishing.net

How I Made $2,000,000 In The Stock Market, Nicolas Darvas, www.bnpublishing.net

www.ingramcontent.com/pod-product-compliance
Lightning Source LLC
Chambersburg PA
CBHW051420200326

41520CB00023B/7309